A Bad Dream

A Play

Simon Brett

A SAMUEL FRENCH ACTING EDITION

SAMUEL FRENCH

FOUNDED 1830

SAMUELFRENCH-LONDON.CO.UK
SAMUELFRENCH.COM

FOR AMATEUR PRODUCTION ENQUIRIES

UNITED KINGDOM AND WORLD EXCLUDING NORTH AMERICA

plays@SamuelFrench-London.co.uk

020 7255 4302/01

Each title is subject to availability from Samuel French,

depending upon country of performance.

A BAD DREAM

First presented by Sutton Amateur Dramatic Club at the Secombe Centre, Sutton, on 12th November 2002, with the following cast:

Miss Brabazon	Anne Page
Mr Galley	Geoff Alldis
Mr Harry Trunchpole	Paul Köhler
The Hon. Montague Pottle	Nicholas Ward
Mr Augustus Tarleton	Roly Adlam
Mr Lawrence Furze	Lewis Wilmott
Miss Florence Horton	Wendy Southall
Miss Lettice Sandwich	Patricia Foley
Mr Branston Parrish	Brian Turner
Mrs Constantia Littlehouse	Jean Manning
Miss Myrtle Throckmorton	Ira Murray
Miss Lydia Farrelly	Susanne Schlaefli
Miss Alberta De Lainey	Tamara Köhler
Miss Amelia De Lainey	Emma Boddy
Miss Arabella De Lainey	Chloe Caselton
Miss Alexandra De Lainey	Sarahjane Neal
Mrs Maud De Lainey	Margaret Hey
Mr Sydney De Lainey	Rob Clark
Miss Daisy Winsom	Annabelle Lawrence
Detective-Sergeant Frobisher	David Gillespie

Directed by Sheila Carr

CHARACTERS

Miss Brabazon, pianist, 40s-50s
Mr Galley, caretaker, 40s-50s
Mr Harry Trunchpole, 20s-30s
The Hon Montague Pottle, "Monty", 20s-30s
Mr Augustus Tarleton, "Gus", 20s-30s
Mr Lawrence Furze, accounts clerk, 20s-30s
Miss Florence Horton, one of the founders of the B.A.D.;
  of "a certain age"
Miss Lettice Sandwich, her sidekick; similar age
Mr Branston Parrish, middle-aged
Mrs Constantia Littlehouse, Founder of the B.A.D., 60s
Miss Myrtle Throckmorton, 30s
Miss Lydia Farrelly, late 20s
Mrs Maud De Lainey, late 40s
Mr Sydney De Lainey, her husband, an entrepreneur;
  40s-50s
Miss Alberta De Lainey, 12
Miss Amelia De Lainey, 14
Miss Arabella De Lainey, 16
Miss Alexandra De Lainey, 18
Miss Daisy Winsom, 12
Detective-Sergeant Frobisher, 30s-40s

SYNOPSIS OF SCENES

The action of the play takes place in the Committee Room
of the Bellingford Jubilee Institute in a London suburb

Time—1902

ACT I

SCENE 1   Tuesday, 17th June
SCENE 2   Tuesday, 24th June

ACT II

SCENE 1   Monday, 15th September
SCENE 2   Tuesday, 12th November

MUSICAL NUMBERS

Bill Bailey, Won't You Please Come Home? — Words and music by Hughie Cannon (Sung by **Lydia Farrelly**, p. 69)

The Boy I Love Is Up in the Gallery — Words and music by George Ware (Sung by **Lydia Farrelly** and **Harry**, p. 16, **Branston Parrish** and **Audience** p. 93)

Funny Things They Do Upon the Sly —Words G.W. Hunt and John Cooke Jnr. Music G.W. Hunt (Sung by **Branston Parrish**, p.56)

A More Humane Mikado (from *The Mikado*) W.S. Gilbert and Arthur Sullivan (Sung by **Branston Parrish**, p.18)

On the Day King Edward Gets his Crown On —Words and music by Mark Lorne and Harry Pleon © Asherberg Hopwood and Crew Ltd, London W6 8BS. Reproduced by permission of International Music Publications Ltd. All Rights Reserved. (Sung by **Mr Galley**, pp. 1-2)

Tuner's Oppor-Tuner-ty —Words Harry Adam, music Fred Coyne (Sung by **Branston Parrish**, p.72)

Up in a Balloon — Words and music by G.W. Hunt (Sung by **Mr Galley**, p. 44)

Up Went the Price — Words and music by George Ware (Sung by **Branston Parrish**, p.78)

What Did She Know about Railways? —C.G. Cotes and Bennett Scott (Sung by **Mr Galley**, p.3)

Whilst every effort has been made to secure permission for quoting the above songs, it has in some cases proven impossible to trace the author or his executor. We apologize for our apparent negligence.

If it proves impossible to find sheet music for any of the songs in this play, directors are at liberty to use other songs from the period.

We would like to thank Patricia Godwin for her assistance with musical copyright research.

Simon Brett

AUTHOR'S NOTE

In the year 2000 I was approached by Dick Bower of the Sutton Amateur Dramatic Club, asking if I might be prepared to write a play to celebrate the group's centenary in 2002. They were offering to commission me; it was all done in a very professional way. I said yes for three reasons. One, Sutton was very near where I was brought up (Banstead in Surrey), and I'd been to a prep school there called Homefield. Two, I was intrigued by the idea of writing something historical (and I'd very quickly decided that the play needed to be set in 1902). And three, I've always loved amateur dramatics — constantly rehearsing for plays had helped me through the agonizing awkwardnesses of adolescence — and I thought the fact that any amateur dramatic society had survived a hundred years was something worthy of celebration.

S.A.D.C. came up with a production, directed by Sheila Carr, with which I was delighted. They understood the fun of the piece, as well as its moments of drama and tension. Every member of the large cast put a hundred per cent into filling the characters I had created.It was a wonderful experience for me — and the company seemed to enjoy it too.

I hope many more amateur dramatic societies will have as much fun with *A Bad Dream* as we did during its first production.

Simon Brett

Other plays by Simon Brett
published by Samuel French Ltd

Mr Quigley's Revenge
Murder in Play
Silhouette
Sleeping Beauty
The Tale of Little Red Riding Hood

ACT I
SCENE 1

The Committee Room of the Bellingford Jubilee Institute. Tuesday 17th June 1902. Evening

The Institute was built in 1887 to commemorate Queen Victoria's Jubilee. The room backs on to the stage of the Institute Hall, which is used for public lectures and amateur dramatics. The Committee Room itself is also hired out for meetings and functions; on this occasion it is being used for the first rehearsal of the Bellingford Amateur Dramaticks' production of "A Midsummer Night's Dream". The décor is ornate, demonstrating the civic pride with which the Victorians invested all their public architecture. But the room has become slightly shabby with heavy use during the fifteen years since its opening

C is a set of double doors. UL and UR are single doors. All of these lead to the backstage area of the Institute Hall. DL is another door, which leads to the entrance lobby. US of this is a window that looks out on to the street. There is a further door DR, which leads to the utility area, kitchen and toilets. Above the double doors, C of the back wall is a large portrait of Queen Victoria in her later years. There are also plaques listing the dignitaries who were present at the Institute's official opening, and a set of wall brackets. The lighting is by gas. The room's furnishings include a large committee table and matching chairs. An upright piano stands against one wall

When the CURTAIN rises, the stage is in darkness

Mr Galley, the caretaker of the Bellingford Jubilee Institute, enters. He is dressed in dark suit trousers, shirt and tie, and a long brown apron and is carrying a lighted taper

During the following, Mr Galley ignites the wall-fitted gas-lights around the room, starting L. As he does so, he sings Harry Pleon's music hall song "On the Day King Edward Gets his Crown On" to himself (though loud enough, of course, for the audience to hear). Mr Galley is not a great singer, but clearly fancies himself as one; he gets more confident and carried away as he gets deeper into the song

The lighting on stage builds up as more gas-lights are lit

Mr Galley (*singing*) There's a good time coming soon for the family
        On the day King Edward gets his crown on.
        Parading up and down the Strand, all of us you'll see,
        On the day King Edward gets his crown on.
        We'll all buy penny ticklers, and won't we have a lark?
        All the p'licemen Mother meets she'll cuddle in the dark,
        Father's going to smack them on their vaccination mark
        On the day King Edward gets his crown on.
        Up and down the Strand ——
        Up and down the Strand ——
        Wait until you hear the trumpets sound;
        Shouting Hip Hurray
        All the blooming day
        When our good King Edward's crowned.

Mr Galley gets more carried away as he sings the second verse. He moves to light the gas-lights R

Miss Brabazon enters though the entrance lobby door. She is a severe spinster lady dressed in dark clothes and wearing a bonnet from a previous generation. She stands looking at Mr Galley with disapproval

Mr Galley does not notice Miss Brabazon's arrival

        Father's going to change his socks and Auntie have a bath,
        On the day King Edward gets his crown on.
        With a brick we'll hit the landlord to make the baby laugh,
        On the day King Edward gets his crown on.
        The lodger's going to get blind drunk, as soon as day
          begins,
        Sister's wearing bloomers fixed up with safety pins …

Mr Galley finishes his task and turns — to be faced by the implacable Miss Brabazon. The words of his song trickle away

        To celebrate the great event — Mother — will — have —
          twins …
Miss Brabazon (*dourly; disapprovingly*) We'll have no talk of "bloomers" here, thank you, Mr Galley.
Mr Galley I'm most sorry, Miss Brabazon. I did not realize there was anyone else present.
Miss Brabazon Evidently.
Mr Galley May I ask to what I owe the pleasure of your company? This evening the Institute is booked for a rehearsal by the Bellingford Amateur

Dramaticks. Surely, Miss Brabazon, we're not about to see you *acting*, are we? I've never thought of you as a classical actress like Ellen Terry or Violet Vanbrugh. A Marie Lloyd or a Vesta Tilley, one of the music hall stars perhaps ...

Miss Brabazon Don't be impertinent, Mr Galley. I am here to play the piano for the Bellingford Amateur Dramaticks.

Mr Galley I thought you only played piano for hymn-singing and Temperance meetings.

Miss Brabazon A spinster lady in my circumstances plays piano for whoever pays her to play piano. So long as it is not an engagement that might compromise my Christian faith.

Mr Galley (*surprised*) Are you telling me that Mrs Littlehouse of the Bellingford Amateur Dramaticks is offering to pay you? I thought they'd run out of money.

Miss Brabazon No, I was offered the engagement by a Mr Sydney De Lainey.

Mr Galley (*recognizing the name, but covering up quickly*) Haven't heard of him. Must be a new member.

Miss Brabazon All I know is that he is prepared to pay for my piano-playing. Which is why I am here, Mr Galley. (*She heads for the exit* DR) Now excuse me, I must go and — explore the facilities.

Mr Galley Yes, and have one for me while you're at it.

Miss Brabazon (*bridling*) Mr Galley! (*Raising an admonitory finger to him*) And no more profane singing.

Mr Galley Of course not. (*He smiles innocently*)

Miss Brabazon makes her magisterial exit

Mr Galley goes slyly into the last line of Marie Lloyd's song, "What Did She Know About Railways?"

Mr Galley And ... (*singing*) " she'd never had a ticket punch'd before". (*He chuckles*)

There are sounds from the entrance lobby of people arriving

Mr Galley turns towards the lobby

Harry (*off*) Come on, chaps! We've got time for a game!

Harry Trunchpole, Monty Pottle and Gus Tarleton come bounding in from the lobby. They are well-heeled young men in their twenties or thirties. Harry is bright, with a lot of charm; Gus takes on the pose of the world-weary cynic; Monty's a bit of a silly ass. Harry carries a box containing a Ping-Pong set

Harry (*seeing the committee table*) Perfect, they've got just the right sort of
    table here. (*He goes straight across to the table, opens the box and sets up
    the Ping-Pong game during the following*)

Monty That's dashed convenient.

Gus Amazing the facilities you find in these suburban slums.

Mr Galley (*offended at this takeover of his premises*) Excuse me, gentlemen.
    May I ask what you are doing here? The Institute has been booked for a
    rehearsal by the Bellingford Amateur Dramaticks.

Gus Which is precisely why we are here. We're going to be in the show.

Monty Yes, we jolly well are.

Mr Galley That's still no reason why you should be placing objects on the
    Committee Room table.

Gus Oh, nuts, Granddad. Mind your own business.

Mr Galley Now, listen, you young cubs ——

Harry (*coming forward to defuse the situation; very smoothly*) Gentlemen,
    gentlemen ... Please let's be civilized about this. (*To Mr Galley*) What's
    your name, my good fellow?

Mr Galley (*defensively*) Mr Galley.

Harry (*reaching over to shake Mr Galley's hand*) I'm Harry Trunchpole.
    Son of Sir Theodore Trunchpole.

Mr Galley (*impressed, in spite of himself*) Sir Theodore ...

Harry and Mr Galley shake hands

Harry Mm. Now, Mr Galley, do you know what Ping-Pong is?

Mr Galley No, I don't, but it sounds foreign, and you can't do it here. Not
    on the Committee Room table. It's against the Institute regulations.
    (*Quoting the regulations*) "No profanity or lewd behaviour is allowed."

Harry Ping-Pong's not profane or lewd. It's just a game.

Mr Galley "The playing of games in the Committee Room is also forbidden."

Harry (*reaching into his pocket and producing a coin*) Are you sure you
    couldn't stretch a point, Mr Galley ...?

Mr Galley No, I'm afraid it's more than my job's worth to ...

Harry pushes the coin into Mr Galley's hand

It's not me, you see, it's the Institute's regulations ... (*Looking down at his
    hand to see what's been put into it*) Oh ... Well, maybe — just this once.
    (*Moving towards the* UR *door*) There are a few things I need to attend to in
    the hall, as it happens. Just mind you don't scratch that table.

Mr Galley exits UR

Harry (*turning triumphantly to his friends*) Never underestimate the power of the well-placed half-crown.

Gus I'd have just told the blighter to shove off.

Harry I'm sure you would, Gus, which is why I will survive better in this new century than you will.

Gus What the devil do you mean?

Harry Socialism is about to triumph, comrade. This will be the century of the working man.

Gus What an absolutely beastly thought.

Monty Look, come on, are we going to play or not?

Harry (*returning to the table and setting up the net*) Yes, of course.

Monty Good egg. I'm an absolute nut for Whiff-Waff.

Harry For what?

Monty Whiff-Waff. We've got a set of this at home, and it's called Whiff-Waff.

Harry It's called Ping-Pong.

Monty Your set's called Ping-Pong. Mine's called Whiff-Waff. I think you'll find most chaps call it Whiff-Waff. You take my word for it — Whiff-Waff's the name that'll survive.

Harry Tommy-rot.

Monty Put money on it. Ten guineas that in ten years' time — when will that be? June the seventeenth 1912 — everyone calls this game Whiff-Waff.

Harry (*shaking Monty's hand*) You're on, Monty. Righty-ho, all set up. Who's going to play first?

Monty I want to have a go. I'm a bit of a dab hand, actually.

Harry You haven't played, have you, Gus?

Gus No. Done lawn tennis, of course. I'll sit this out and watch.

Harry You'll soon get the idea. (*Taking the bats out of the box*) You see, the battledores are just like miniature lawn tennis ones. (*He takes a celluloid ball out of the box and bounces it on the table*)

Gus (*intrigued by the sound*) What's that made of?

Harry Celluloid — you know, stuff they use to make collars for clerks.

Gus (*impressed*) The deuce it is.

Harry Shift-ho, Monty. Let's start.

Monty Good business.

Harry You can serve. (*He bounces the ball across the table to Monty*)

Monty I always beat my mater hands down at this. She says she wouldn't be surprised if I end up as the World Champion at Whiff-Waff.

Harry Though maybe not at Ping-Pong. Anyway, we'll see. Love-all.

They play. In spite of what he's said, Monty is absolutely rubbish at the game. Harry easily has the measure of him. During the following, there are few rallies, and Monty spends most of the game retrieving the ball from the furthest corners of the room. After the first couple of points, Harry finds he can easily continue a conversation with Gus, and still beat Monty hands-down

Monty serves

Harry (*returning the service with a smash*) One-love.
Monty (*retrieving the ball*) Blow! You caught me on the hop there. Don't worry, I'll try my special service.

Monty does an over-elaborate serve, which Harry returns with another almost contemptuous smash

(*Retrieving the ball*) Oh, dash it!
Harry Two-love.
Gus What's all this really about, Harry?
Harry Gus, we're taking part in Amateur Dramatics, that's all. I met this cove Sydney De Lainey – he said he was short of men for his production of *A Midsummer Night's Dream*.

Monty serves again

(*Smashing the ball*) Three-love. I said I could find him some chaps from my club — here we are.
Gus I said what's it *really* about?

Monty serves; Harry returns the ball with interest. Monty, looking a bit lugubrious, has to go the far side of the room to retrieve the ball

Harry Four-love. (*To Gus*) No more than that, old fellow.
Gus (*moving closer to Harry; almost whispering*) You said it might be a way of getting me out of this beastly hole I'm in.
Monty (*coming back to the table*) I was going to keep this service up my sleeve for a while — it always foxes Mater — but you've asked for it, Harry.

Monty performs another even more elaborate serve. Harry smashes it back with indolent ease

Oh, rats!
Harry Five-love.

Monty moves away to retrieve the ball

Harry (*turning back to Gus and almost whispering*) Listen, Gus. My good friend De Lainey has got pots of the old spondulicks.

Gus Inherited?

Harry No, he worked for it.

Gus (*dismissively*) Oh.

Monty (*returning to the table and bouncing the ball across the table to Harry*) Your serve then.

Harry Righty-ho. (*He serves past Monty*)

Monty retrieves the ball yet again during the following

Monty Oh, double rats!

Harry Six-love. (*To Gus*) De Lainey made his killing in African diamonds ——

Gus (*even more dismissively*) Really?

Harry — and he has a marriageable daughter.

Gus (*interested now*) Ah.

Monty (*returning the ball to Harry*) Enough of this shilly-shallying. I'm really going to try now.

Harry Splendid news. (*He serves straight past Monty*) Seven-love.

Monty (*going to collect the ball*) This is beastly. I'm being mopped. (*He finds the ball and crouches to pick it up*)

Lawrence Furze enters from the lobby, carrying two books and wearing a hat which he removes. Lawrence is about the same age as the other young men, and good-looking, but of a very different class. He wears a cheap business suit, and looks like the accounts clerk that he is. His manner is earnest and nervous, and his voice doesn't have the upper-crust gloss of the other three young men

Monty looks up from the floor. He sees Lawrence and rises

Lawrence (*to Monty, as he rises*) Hallo. Is this the right place for the Bellingford Amateur Dramaticks?

Monty Spot on. Sorry, must get back to the game. (*He returns to the table, speaking over his shoulder*) Are you a nut for Whiff-Waff?

Lawrence I beg your pardon?

But Monty has already gone back to the game, which continues in silence, except for Harry calling out the score, as he continues to win every point

Lawrence looks at the other young men, but gets no response, so he goes awkwardly across to sit on a chair DL. He opens one of his books and gives the impression that he's reading it, though he clearly isn't

After a while, Gus, who has been idly watching the game of Ping-Pong, strolls down towards Lawrence

Gus (*patronizingly*) You here for this *Midsummer Night's Dream* caper, are you?

Lawrence Yes. I've got the part of Lys-s-sander.

Gus Ah. And how do you come to be involved?

Lawrence I'm an accounts clerk in Mr De Lainey's office.

Gus (*without enthusiasm*) Are you?

Lawrence My name's Lawrence Furze.

Gus Is it?

Lawrence (*once he realizes Gus is not about to volunteer his name*) And I'm doing Amateur Dramatics to overcome my s ... s-s-s-s-s-stammer.

Gus Hasn't done the trick yet, has it? (*He smiles sardonically and ambles back to watch the Ping-Pong*)

Harry is just finishing his trouncing of Monty

Harry Look, Monty old chap, I'm getting a bit bored with this. You're never going to get a point, so let's call it a day. (*Or, if the timing works*: Twenty-love. My game, I think, Monty old chap.)

Monty The trouble is, I'm not entirely used to a table like this. And the battledores we have at home for Whiff-Waff are a little different.

Harry Are you going to have a shot, Gus?

Monty Oh, come on, Harry. You've got to let me have my revenge first.

Harry (*ignoring Monty*) Gus?

Gus In a little while. Need a smoke first. I'm absolutely gasping for a cigarette.

Harry (*producing a cigarette case*) Yes, I could do with one. Better not in here.

Harry leads Gus towards the exit DR

Wonder if a hole like this actually has a smoking-room. Let's have a look.

Harry and Gus exit

Monty (*trailing after them*) I thought we were meant to be playing Whiff-Waff.

Monty exits

Lawrence gets up tentatively and goes across to look at the Ping-Pong equipment on the table. He has never seen it before, and is intrigued. He picks up one of the bats and prepares to hit the ball. Then he hears the clatter of the outside door; he hurries back across to his seat and picks up his book

Miss Florence Horton and Miss Lettice Sandwich enter from the lobby. They are both members of the Bellingford Amateur Dramaticks; the former, one of the founders, is a redoubtable lady of a certain age; the latter, a more recent recruit, is her twittery and self-effacing sidekick. Both have copies of the play

Lawrence rises rather awkwardly. The women ignore him, so he soon sits down again

Miss Horton (*looking at the equipment on the table*) Is there nowhere in the country one can go to avoid the wretched Ping-Pong?
Miss Sandwich It is remarkably popular, is it not, Miss Horton?

Miss Horton looks magisterially around the room and sees Lawrence

Miss Horton (*in a loud whisper*) A new face for the Bellingford Amateur Dramaticks. I hope he will soon learn our little ways.
Miss Sandwich (*also in a loud whisper*) Oh, I'm sure he will, Miss Horton.

Miss Horton doesn't look entirely convinced about this. There is a silence

Hem, I was thinking ...
Miss Horton Well, don't, Miss Sandwich. It doesn't suit you.
Miss Sandwich (*after a little nervous throat-clearing*) No, I was wondering why the Dramaticks had chosen *A Midsummer Night's Dream*. The play has such a large cast, and surely the scenery and dresses will be very costly. I thought we lost a lot of money on our production of *School*.
Miss Horton We did. In spite of my own fine performance.
Miss Sandwich Then where will the money come from for this production?
Miss Horton Ah. Mrs Littlehouse has a new source of funds.
Miss Sandwich Indeed?
Miss Horton She has met a money-bags from the diamond trade.
Miss Sandwich Oh?
Miss Horton A Mr De Lainey, who is a great enthusiast of amateur dramatics — and also a great enthusiast of Henry Irving.
Miss Sandwich *Sir* Henry Irving we must say now.
Miss Horton Yes. To think we have lived to the day when an actor can be knighted. Every thing is topsy-turvy now. Dukes' sons marry American heiresses. The daughters of industrialists pay their way into the peerage. (*She looks up at the picture of Queen Victoria*) The late Queen must be spinning in her grave like a gyroscope. Knighthoods for *actors* — whatever next?
Miss Sandwich Of course it was Queen Victoria who knighted Sir Henry, Miss Horton.

Miss Horton That doesn't change my point about the general collapse of civilized society.

Miss Sandwich And, anyway, Sir Henry Irving is so much more than an actor. He is a phenomenon. (*Fondly remembering*) You know, I saw Sir Henry Irving in *Much Ado About Nothing* back in '84. He was a magnificent Benedick. And Miss Ellen Terry a wonderful Beatrice.

Miss Horton Yes ... Though many people were of the view that my performance in the part for the Bellingford Amateur Dramaticks was better.

Miss Sandwich Oh, of course, of course. Both performances were excellent.

Miss Horton looks sternly at Miss Sandwich

Though yours, perhaps, the more excellent.

Miss Horton (*gratified*) Hm ... It would seem that Mrs Littlehouse is late again.

Miss Sandwich Yes. (*Looking down at her copy of the play*) Mrs Littlehouse wishes me to play the part of Flute, the Bellows-mender.

Miss Horton That is very appropriate. It is a small part, Miss Sandwich. Even you cannot get it too far wrong.

Miss Sandwich That was not my concern, Miss Horton. I am worried by the fact that Flute the Bellows-mender is a *masculine* part.

Miss Horton You must know that in all amateur dramatic societies, there are more ladies than gentlemen, and often a lady will have to take a masculine part. Where is your anxiety?

Miss Sandwich (*embarrassed*) It is ... I am afraid that I may be expected to — wear — trousers.

Miss Horton Nonsense. The dresses for the play of *A Midsummer Night's Dream* will be of the Athenian period, long before the invention of trousering.

Miss Sandwich Oh, thank heavens, Miss Horton. (*Silence*) So what would have been worn by a bellows-mender of the Athenian period?

Miss Horton A tunic.

Miss Sandwich A tunic? (*Silence*) And how far down the ... er, anatomy would such a tunic extend?

Miss Horton To just below the knee.

Miss Sandwich (*appalled*) Miss Horton!

Branston Parrish enters from the lobby. He is another regular of the Bellingford Amateur Dramaticks, a middle-aged man dressed in a loud check suit, carrying a copy of the The Times *under his arm. Though liking to give the impression that he has connections with the professional stage and music hall, he is, in fact, by trade a grocer. Between him and Miss Horton there exists a state of mutual loathing*

Branston Parrish nods to Lawrence, who looks up nervously from his book.
Branston Parrish then takes his hat off to the two ladies

Branston Parrish Miss Horton, good-evening.
Miss Horton Mr Parrish. You haven't met Miss Sandwich.
Branston Parrish I have not had that pleasure. (*Taking Miss Sandwich's
hand flamboyantly*) Branston Parrish at your service. Leading actor of the
Bellingford Amateur Dramaticks.
Miss Horton And by day a grocer.

Branston Parrish looks miffed

Miss Sandwich is also a member of the Society, Mr Parrish. She took a part
in our recent production of Tom Robertson's *School*.
Branston Parrish Which is why I have not met her. There were no suitable
roles for me in that play.
Miss Horton No. Mr Robertson did not write for low comedians.
Branston Parrish (*deliberately not rising to this*) But fortunately there is an
excellent part for me in *A Midsummer Night's Dream*. One that I have
wished to play for my entire career.
Miss Sandwich And what is that, Mr Parrish?
Branston Parrish Bottom.
Miss Sandwich Oh. (*She gives a nervous, embarrassed giggle*)
Branston Parrish Bottom is a vainglorious buffoon in a group of amateur
actors, who tries to take all the best parts for himself
Miss Horton You might start with a slight advantage in your interpretation
of the role, Mr Parrish.
Branston Parrish (*as if he hasn't heard this*) Will be hard for me to play so
against type, but then that's the challenge of acting. I'll think of it as a
character part. (*Looking beadily at Miss Horton*) I'm surprised there was
a suitable role for you, Miss Horton. What are you — an Attendant Lady?
Miss Horton I am Hippolyta ——
Branston Parrish Indeed?
Miss Horton —— Queen of the Amazons.
Branston Parrish (*sitting down and opening his newspaper*) A monstrous
battleaxe. What perfect casting.
Miss Horton (*annoyed*) Mr Parrish ——
Branston Parrish (*overriding Miss Horton*) All seems to be set fair for the
King's Coronation next week.
Miss Sandwich Oh, indeed. That will be a day the like of which we have not
witnessed since the Jubilee of the late Queen ... (*She looks up to the picture
on the back wall*) God rest her soul.
Branston Parrish Good that the war's ended in time for the Coronation.
(*Referring to his newspaper*) Sixteen and a half thousand of the Boer troops

have now surrendered. Soon lost the stomach for the fight, didn't they? Long live the Empire, eh?

Lawrence (*unable to keep quiet*) Yes. Long live the Empire, as long as it is a humane empire.

Branston Parrish What?

Lawrence (*rising from his seat and moving to the others*) My name is Lawrence Furze.

Branston Parrish I don't give a damn what your name is. What did you say?

Lawrence I said, "Long live the Empire, so long as it is a humane Empire."

Branston Parrish And what the devil do you mean by that?

Lawrence I mean we should not be proud of everything done by our s-s-soldiers in S-S-South Africa. Kitchener's "s-s-s-scorched earth" policy caused great distress to many ——

Branston Parrish Look, it was a war. They were enemies. Things happen in wartime.

Lawrence The cruelty to women and children cannot be condoned. I heard a lecture on the s-s-subject by Mrs Emily Hobhouse and ——

Branston Parrish Never heard of her. What is she – one of these "New Women"? All smoking cigarettes and reckoning she's got enough brains to vote?

Lawrence She is someone who cares for ——

Branston Parrish (*overriding him*) At least thank God you're not one of these "New Women", are you, Miss Horton?

Miss Horton Certainly not!

Branston Parrish (*finding the following joke very funny*) No, you're very definitely an "Old Woman"!

Miss Horton (*not finding this at all funny*) Mr Parrish, I will ask you to keep a civil tongue in your head!

Mrs Constantia Littlehouse, Miss Myrtle Throckmorton and Miss Lydia Farrelly enter, interrupting the spat. Mrs Littlehouse, Founder of the Bellingford Amateur Dramaticks, is a scatterbrained, rather ineffectual woman; Myrtle Throckmorton is large, clumsy, but very willing; and Lydia Farrelly is tall, extremely sexy and probably more knowing than an Edwardian lady of her age (late twenties) should be

Branston Parrish rises to his feet as the ladies enter

Miss Horton Ah, Mrs Littlehouse. You have arrived at last. Now perhaps finally we may begin some work.

Mrs Littlehouse Good-evening, Miss Horton. Miss Sandwich. Apologies for my tardiness. I got delayed on the omnibus. You know Miss Throckmorton, of course?

Miss Horton Of course. Good-evening, Myrtle.

Myrtle Throckmorton (*with a clumsy curtsy*) Good-evening.

Mrs Littlehouse And Miss Farrelly …

Miss Horton (*frostily; she disapproves of Miss Lydia Farrelly*) Good-evening.

Branston Parrish (*moving across to greet Mrs Littlehouse in an elaborately over-the-top manner*) Good-evening, Constantia. How your radiant presence illuminates even the murky darknesses of the Bellingford Jubilee Institute!

Mrs Littlehouse (*simpering*) Oh, Branston, what a complete ass you are.

Miss Horton (*to Miss Sandwich, sotto voce*) I myself have never been in favour of elaborate compliments.

Branston Parrish overhears this

Branston Parrish Just as well, Miss Horton — since you are never likely to receive any.

Miss Horton looks daggers at Branston Parrish

Mrs Littlehouse Has Mr De Lainey arrived?

Branston Parrish We have not seen him. (*Looking at Lawrence*) Unless this *pacifist* gentleman is ——

Lawrence I told you.

Lydia Farrelly notices Lawrence for the first time. She likes what she sees

My name is Lawrence Furze and ——

Miss Horton (*interrupting*) So tell me, Mrs Littlehouse, who exactly is this Mr De Lainey?

Mrs Littlehouse My dear Miss Horton, Sydney De Lainey is no less than the complete salvation of the Bellingford Amateur Dramaticks. A man deeply immersed in all things theatrical …

Miss Horton And all things commercial, I gather.

Mrs Littlehouse He has indeed made a considerable fortune as a diamond merchant. (*Excitedly*) And he has agreed to pay for all the settings and dresses for our production of *A Midsummer Night's Dream*.

Branston Parrish Which part is he to play?

Mrs Littlehouse Oberon, King of the Fairies.

Miss Horton And I gather he will play it in the manner of Henry Irving?

Mrs Littlehouse *Sir* Henry. Oh, indeed yes. Mr De Lainey is a great devotee of Sir Henry's work.

Miss Horton And you are certain he will cause no disruption to the way we manage our affairs in the Bellingford Amateur Dramaticks?

Mrs Littlehouse None at all, I'm sure of it.

Lydia Farrelly Then he will be very different from the real Henry Irving.

Mrs Littlehouse I beg your pardon? Oh yes, of course. Lydia — Miss Farrelly — was actually in Sir Henry's company at the Lyceum.

Miss Horton (*frostily*) In very minor roles, though, I gather.

Lydia Farrelly Everyone is in very minor roles in Henry Irving's company. The brightest light is always on him — "the Guv'nor" as he likes to be called — on him both literally and metaphorically. Henry Irving is egotism personified.

Myrtle Throckmorton Oh, but he is such a romantic figure. When I was a small child, my father took me to see Irving as Hamlet. I have never forgotten it. He is my ideal of the romantic hero.

Branston Parrish Kind of man you'd like to end up married to, Miss Throckmorton?

Myrtle Throckmorton (*carried away*) Oh, yes, yes.

Branston Parrish Well, I think you might have a long wait.

Myrtle Throckmorton gives Branston Parrish a sour look

Miss Sandwich But there is no doubt at all that Sir Henry Irving is a very fine actor.

Lawrence (*once again unable to keep quiet*) I cannot agree. His acting is all postures and mannerisms. George Bernard Shaw wrote of Henry Irving in the *S-S-S-Saturday Review* that he ——

Branston Parrish Please! We don't want to hear the views of beastly Socialists like George Bernard Shaw in the Bellingford Amateur Dramaticks.

Miss Horton No, we most certainly don't.

Miss Horton and Branston Parrish exchange a look of surprised puzzlement. They've actually agreed on something for once

Lawrence George Bernard Shaw wrote that Henry Irving does not merely cut the plays he produces: he disembowels them.

Branston Parrish I do not wish to hear again the name of George Bernard Shaw — or of any other Irishman, come to that! Filthy bogtrotters!

Lawrence You cannot dismiss a whole s-s-s-society of ——

Mrs Littlehouse Please, please, gentlemen. We want no arguments.

Branston Parrish But if the young bounder insists on ——

Mrs Littlehouse (*putting her hand on Branston's arm to calm him*) Please, Branston. For me.

Branston Parrish (*calming down and going into flattery mode*) Oh. Well. For you, Constantia — how can I refuse? When I see the appeal in those

dashed sparklin', ravishin' eyes ... When I'm aware of all those endearin'
young charms ...

Mrs Littlehouse (*simpering*) Oh, Branston ...

Miss Horton (*nauseated*) Oh, dear ...

Mrs Littlehouse (*clapping her hands*) Now come on, please, we must get
down to some work. Are we the only people here?

Lawrence There were some other fellows earlier.

Mrs Littlehouse Oh, they are probably the young men Mr De Lainey has
drummed up for me.

Lawrence (*pointing off* R) They went through there. (*During the following
he returns to his seat and his book*)

Mrs Littlehouse Well, could somebody go and fetch them?

Myrtle Throckmorton Shall I go, Constantia?

Mrs Littlehouse No, Myrtle. I want you to come with me to the Hall. I think
we might find Mr Galley there, and I need to have a word with him.

Myrtle Throckmorton Very well, Constantia.

Branston Parrish I'll come with you too. That Mr Galley's got wandering
hands, and I don't want them wandering over you, my speck of angel-dust.

Mrs Littlehouse (*simpering*) Oh, Branston, what tommy-rot you talk.
(*Moving towards the* UR *door and calling over her shoulder*) Could you
fetch the others, Miss Horton?

*Mrs Littlehouse, Branston Parrish and Myrtle Throckmorton exit though
by the* UR *door*

Miss Horton Huh. What does she think I am — some little slavey?

*Lydia Farrelly saunters towards the piano. Miss Horton and Miss Sandwich
become very aware of her. During the ensuing dialogue, Lydia Farrelly sits
down at the keyboard and starts to pick out the tune of "The Boy I Love Is Up
in the Gallery"*

Miss Horton (*looking beadily at Lydia and speaking in a stage whisper*) I
was never in favour of the employment of actresses in the Bellingford
Amateur Dramaticks.

Miss Sandwich (*also in a stage whisper*) What, Miss Horton, you favour the
playing of all the parts by gentlemen?

Miss Horton No, Miss Sandwich. I mean, I do not think we should have
professional actresses in our society.

Miss Sandwich Why not, Miss Horton?

Miss Horton A professional actress is not a respectable person. (*Darkly*)
And the presence of a professional actress might give the men ideas.

Miss Sandwich Oh. (*Silence*) But an *amateur* actress is a respectable person?

Miss Horton (*crushingly*) Of course, Miss Sandwich.

Miss Sandwich Of course. (*Silence*) Miss Farrelly no longer acts for her living. She is a *former* professional actress.

Miss Horton So far as I'm concerned, Miss Sandwich, that makes the situation worse rather than better.

Miss Sandwich Oh.

Miss Horton leads Miss Sandwich towards the DR *exit*

Miss Horton Come on, we'd better go and perform our errand for Mrs Littlehouse.

Miss Horton and Miss Sandwich exit

Lydia Farrelly is well aware that she and Lawrence are the only ones left in the Committee Room. She flashes a flirtatious look at him, which he pretends not to see. Then she starts playing and singing the chorus of "The Boy I Love Is Up in the Gallery", doing it, at this point, for Lawrence's benefit

Harry Trunchpole enters DR *a little way through the song*

Harry smiles at Lydia Farrelly, who responds. Then he joins in singing with her. Lawrence is forgotten

Lydia Farrelly (*singing*)   The boy I love is up in the gallery
                                    The boy I love is looking now at me
Lydia Farrelly ⎫   There he is, can't you see?
Harry ⎭   Waving his handkerchief
                                    As merry as a robin
                                    That sings on the tree.

Harry applauds Lydia Farrelly's performance, and they both laugh

Harry You sing it even better than Miss Nelly Power.

Lydia Farrelly inclines her head in gratitude for the compliment. He holds out his hand

   Harry Trunchpole.

Lydia Farrelly (*shaking his hand*) Lydia Farrelly.

Harry Enchanted. What a sight to brighten up a summer's evening.

Lydia Farrelly Thank you, kind sir.

Harry Dash it, I get the feeling we've somehow met before.

Lydia Farrelly You might have seen me on the stage.
Harry (*to whom this means something about the kind of woman she is*) On
the stage, eh? Music hall stage? Musical comedy? Farce?
Lydia Farrelly (*well aware of the innuendo*) I do a bit of everything.
Harry (*also aware of it*) That's deuced good to know. And are you here for
the *Midsummer Night's Dream* lark?
Lydia Farrelly Yes, I'm playing Helena.
Harry The tall, fiery one.
Lydia Farrelly That's for you to find out, Mr Trunchpole.
Harry (*quite sexily*) Harry, please.

They look at each other with mocking intensity

Mrs Littlehouse, Myrtle Throckmorton and Mr Galley enter UR

Lydia Farrelly and Harry break eye contact

Mrs Littlehouse (*to Harry*) Oh, good-evening. We haven't met.
Harry Harry Trunchpole.
Mrs Littlehouse I'm Mrs Constantia Littlehouse. Are you one of the
gentlemen Mr De Lainey organized?
Harry I am. Apparently he wants me to play Demetrius.
Mrs Littlehouse Excellent. I am sorry to have been a little late. There was
a problem on the omnibus.
Harry Ah well, those who travel by omnibus must take the consequences.
What, the traffic, was it?
Mrs Littlehouse A horse died.
Harry Deuced inconsiderate. Dumb animals and servants never think of
others, do they?
Mrs Littlehouse Erm, no. Mr Trunchpole ...
Harry Harry, please.
Mrs Littlehouse Mr Harry Trunchpole — Miss Myrtle Throckmorton.
Harry Good-evening.
Myrtle Throckmorton (*embarrassed*) Good-evening.
Mrs Littlehouse And this is Mr Galley. Harry Trunchpole.
Mr Galley I know. (*With a wink*) Son of Sir Theodore Trunchpole.
Myrtle Throckmorton (*impressed*) Really?
Mr Galley And a dab hand at Pong-Ping.
Harry Ping-Pong.
Mr Galley Exactly.

Miss Horton, Miss Sandwich, Miss Brabazon, Gus and Monty enter from
DR

Mrs Littlehouse (*clapping her hands rather feebly*) Right. Most of us are here, so I think we should make a start. Let's gather round the table and then we can do our introductions. Gentlemen, maybe we could move the table over this way a little?

Branston Parrish Your wish, dear lady, is our command. No sooner said than done. (*Seeing the Ping-Pong equipment*) What the devil's this?

Monty It's for Whiff-Waff.

Harry Or rather for Ping-Pong.

Branston Parrish Ping-Pong? Sounds like something out of *The Mikado*.

During the following song the men manhandle the table to the R of the stage and Harry puts the Ping-Pong equipment back in its box

Branston Parrish fancies himself as a singer, but actually isn't very good

Branston Parrish (*singing; from "The Mikado"*)
            My object all sublime
            I shall achieve in time;
            To let the punishment fit the crime,
            The punishment fit the crime ...

Mrs Littlehouse Thank you very much, gentlemen. Now, if you'd all bring up chairs and sit down.

Gus Where do we sit?

Mrs Littlehouse There's no order or seating plan. We're very informal here at the B.A.D. Just bring a chair and take a place, anywhere.

Everyone takes a chair and finds a place around the table during the following. Instinctively, they take their seats according to gender, the men down one side, the women down the other. Mrs Littlehouse and Branston Parrish sit side by side at the head of the table

I think we'd better get on. Mr De Lainey must be delayed. Maybe there was a problem with his omnibus ...?

Harry Mrs Littlehouse, I don't think you'd catch Mr De Lainey in an omnibus.

Mrs Littlehouse Oh?

Harry No. He'll arrive in a motor car.

They all react, impressed

Mrs Littlehouse Well, goodness me.

Branston Parrish Mr De Lainey must be ... (*singing*) "The man who broke the bank at Monte Carlo."

Harry Oh, I think he's rather wealthier than that. More in the league of that American cove John Pierpoint Morgan.

Branston Parrish (*impressed*) Really?

Everyone is in place by this point

Mrs Littlehouse (*clapping her hands*) Now, ladies and gentlemen, let us set about realizing our *Dream*. As I say, we at the Bellingford Amateur Dramaticks — or B.A.D. for short — are very informal ... One might even use the word "Bohemian" ——

There is a daring giggle from the older ladies

— so we'll dispense with proper introductions. I know some of us are already acquainted, but we'll just go round the table and give our names and the part we're playing in *A Midsummer Night's Dream* — if you don't mind such a casual approach ...

The older ladies again find this a bit daring

— so I will start with myself. Mrs Constantia Littlehouse, Founder of the Bellingford Amateur Dramaticks. I will be acting as the director of the play.
Branston Parrish My name is Branston Parrish. I have played many leading roles for the Bellingford Amateur Dramaticks. I have been right at the top — but now I am Bottom.

A titter goes around the table. Branston Parrish is also amused; he'd set up the line deliberately

Mr Galley Mr Galley. My job is as caretaker of the Bellingford Jubilee Institute. I have in the past been employed by the Bellingford Amateur Dramaticks, using my skills as a stage-carpenter — (*looking pointedly at Mrs Littlehouse*) but nobody's asked me yet this time.
Harry Harry Trunchpole. Demetrius. And these two reprobates are a couple of chaps who're members of my club.
Gus Augustus Tarleton. Theseus.
Monty The Honourable Montague Pottle. Known to all and sundry as "Monty". Apparently, I'm playing someone called "Duck".
Mrs Littlehouse Puck.
Monty Ah. What kind of a fellow is he?
Mrs Littlehouse He's a fairy.
Monty Oh, crikey. Still, don't worry. I'm very good at learning lines. My mater says I've got a memory like a Kodak.

Nobody seems very impressed by this news

Lawrence Lawrence Furze. Lys-s-sander.
Lydia Farrelly Lydia Farrelly. Helena.
Miss Sandwich Lettice Sandwich ...

Harry, Monty and Gus all snigger at this

Branston Parrish And a couple of pickled onions!

The men snigger again

Miss Sandwich (*who has heard these jokes from schooldays on*) My name
is Lettice Sandwich, and I am playing the part of Flute. The Bellows-
mender.
Miss Horton Florence Horton. Hippolyta ... (*Looking challengingly at
Branston Parrish*) Queen of the Amazons.
Branston Parrish I say nothing.
Miss Brabazon Miss Violet Brabazon. I play the piano ——
Mr Galley For whoever pays you to play the piano.
Miss Brabazon (*glaring at Mr Galley*) And I will play any music at all, so
long as it is not profane.
Myrtle Throckmorton I am Myrtle Throckmorton. (*Proudly*) I play the part
of Mustardseed.
Mrs Littlehouse And act as prompter.
Myrtle Throckmorton (*dismayed*) Constantia, do I still have to prompt now
I've got a speaking part?
Mrs Littlehouse Yes, you do.
Myrtle Throckmorton (*downcast*) Oh dear.
Mrs Littlehouse Good. We've now introduced everyone. There are a few
characters still to come. Some are being played by members of the De
Lainey family, and others we still need to find. A bit short of "rude
mechanicals" at the moment.
Miss Sandwich What is a "rude mechanical"?
Mrs Littlehouse You are a "rude mechanical", Lettice.
Miss Sandwich (*offended*) I beg your pardon?
Mrs Littlehouse The "rude mechanicals" are Bottom's friends, the ones
who do the play of *Pyramus and Thisbe*.
Branston Parrish But, O star of my twilight horizon, they're meant to be
men. Miss Sandwich, I can't help noticing, ain't a man.
Mrs Littlehouse (*flirting with Branston Parrish*) I am well aware that Miss
Sandwich is not a man.
Branston Parrish Then please tell me, Constantia ... will my other fellow-
actors in *Pyramus and Thisbe* also be of the feminine gender?
Mrs Littlehouse It depends entirely on who we can find to take the parts.

Branston Parrish (*slightly taken aback*) Oh.

Mrs Littlehouse Don't worry, Branston. We have plenty of time. Our first performance is not until the twelfth of November. You may rely on me to find you some adequately "rude mechanicals".

Branston Parrish I never doubted it for a minute, fair dewdrop on the floweret of dawn.

Mrs Littlehouse (*simpering*) Branston ...

Branston Parrish Constantia ...

Miss Horton (*who's had about as much of this as she can take*) Charming though this undoubtedly may be — don't you think we should be proceeding with our rehearsal?

Mrs Littlehouse Certainly. Of course. I would like to commence by saying a few words about the play, that fragile craft on which our entire company is embarking for a journey to who knows what delights. *A Midsummer Night's Dream* is one of the merriest plays written by William Shakespeare.

During the following, the sound is heard of a 1902 motor car approaching from L. Gradually through the speech, the attention of the group around the table is drawn in that direction

Even though our performance will take place in a cold and frosty November, we want to fill our audience's minds with thoughts of summer and sunshine, of young lovers, of magic and the mystery of fairyland ...

But no-one's listening. They're all looking towards the entrance

I see I might as well be talking to myself.

Monty rushes across the room and looks out of the window

Monty By Jove! It's a spanking new Packard! What a scorcher!

The offstage car brakes and stops. Its engine noise ceases

By now no-one at the table is taking any notice of Mrs Littlehouse. The men drift towards the window, and even some of the women — notably Lydia Farrelly — rise from their seats

There is a silence of anticipation

Monty peers out through the door to the lobby

They're just taking their coats off. I say, the fellow's wearing one of those fancy new Panama hats.

Silence

The four De Lainey daughters enter in age and height sequence, followed by Mrs Maud De Lainey, a well-upholstered woman in her late forties. All are dressed in dresses of the same colour (ideally a pale mauve). They stand in a line from the door, furthest from it Alberta (aged 12 — or younger, if possible), then Amelia (aged 14), Arabella (aged 16, very pretty), Alexandra (aged 18, petite, extremely pretty, rather earnest); then Maud De Lainey nearest the door

A long silence

Sydney De Lainey enters. He has taken modelling himself on Henry Irving to extremes. He tries to look like his idol, and to speak like his idol. He even uses the little dancing steps much noticed by reviewers of Irving's performances. He comes in through the door, sweeps off his Panama hat, and strikes a dramatic pose

Sydney De Lainey (*with gestures*) God-evening, wonn and allll. I em Sydney De Lainey.

Mrs Littlehouse (*stepping forward*) Good-evening. How extremely pleasant to see you again, Mr De Lainey.

Sydney De Lainey (*darting forward to Mrs Littlehouse*) The pleasure, Messes Littlehoss, is all menn. Let me tek your hend.

Mrs Littlehouse (*offering her hand*) Yes, of course.

Sydney De Lainey takes Mrs Littlehouse's hand and, with an elaborate gesture, plants a kiss on it. Mrs Littlehouse simpers, and looks across to see if Branston Parrish is jealous. He is, a little. Sydney De Lainey then holds Mrs Littlehouse at arm's length and gestures to his family

Sydney De Lainey Entroductions. Me femmily. First me dutters. Stutting from the youngest. Ulberta, playing Cobweb.

Alberta (*curtsying*) Good-evening, Mrs Littlehouse.

Sydney De Lainey Ummelia, playing Moth.

Amelia (*curtsying*) Good-evening, Mrs Littlehouse.

Sydney De Lainey Urabella, playing Pizzblossom.

Arabella (*curtsying*) Good-evening, Mrs Littlehouse.

Sydney De Lainey Ulexundra, playing Hermiah.

Alexandra (*curtsying*) Good-evening, Mrs Littlehouse.

Sydney De Lainey And me wuff.

Maud Good-evening, Mrs Littlehouse.

Sydney De Lainey Mod.

Mrs Littlehouse Mod?

Maud Maud.

Mrs Littlehouse Oh, Maud. Yes.

Sydney De Lainey Mod will tek the putt of Titania, and will also be directing the ballets.

Branston Parrish Ballets? There aren't any dashed ballets in *A Midsummer Night's Dream*.

Sydney De Lainey Thar wull be in *may* production. (*Looking around the room*) Ull be demmed if a play can be produced in har.

Mrs Littlehouse No, no. The theatre — the Hall — is through there. Mr Galley here is the caretaker. He's a tower of strength. He knows all about the Institute.

Sydney De Lainey Uh. God, god. Thut is exsullent.

Mr Galley (*awkwardly*) Good-evening, Mr De Lainey.

Sydney De Lainey God-evening. (*Looking at Mr Galley rather curiously*) Hev we nut met befarr, Mr Galliah?

Mr Galley (*slightly evasively*) I don't believe so.

Sydney De Lainey (*still not convinced*) No. Mebbee not. (*He puts the thought from his mind*) So the stedge is through thar ...?

Mrs Littlehouse Perhaps you would like to meet the rest of the company ...?

Sydney De Lainey No. Farst things farst. Farst I must see the stedge, where we are to perform our *Midsummer Nate's Drim*.

Mr Galley If you like to follow me, sir ...

Sydney De Lainey (*leading the way*) Mod! Dutters! Follow me to see the stedge. "Come wonn, come allll. Come see wut doth befallll!"

During the following, Mr Galley leads Sydney De Lainey through the back doors into the Hall. Carried along by Sydney De Lainey's personality, all the rest of the characters follow him off, Lawrence and Alexandra at the back of the crowd

(*As he disappears*) "Ull the world's a stedge,
                                And ull the men and women marley plaaars ..."

Lawrence seems to make a decision; he moves back to the chair where he's left his book. Alexandra, seeing him go, is curious and detaches herself from the crowd. Lawrence does not see her, but picks up his books and makes to leave

Alexandra Where are you going?

Lawrence (*embarrassed*) I ... I must leave.

Alexandra I've seen you before, haven't I?

Lawrence Possibly, Miss De Lainey. I work in your father's office.

Alexandra Oh yes, I have seen you when I've visited him, Mr Furze.
Lawrence How do you know my name?
Alexandra I asked my father. You are called Lawrence Furze.
Lawrence Yes. I'm only an accounts clerk.
Alexandra So what does that matter?
Lawrence I did not expect to hear such words from you, Miss De Lainey.
They sound dangerously like S-S-S-S-S-S ——
Alexandra (*gently helping Lawrence out*) Socialism?
Lawrence Yes.
Alexandra And what is wrong with Socialism?
Lawrence I think there is nothing wrong with S-S-S-S-S-S ——
Alexandra Socialism.
Lawrence Yes. But I wouldn't have expected s-someone with a father like
yours to like the idea.
Alexandra My father detests it above all things. But I don't have to think
what my father thinks.
Lawrence No?
Alexandra (*taking one of Lawrence's books from him and looking at the
title*) Fabian Essays in Socialism. I respect your taste, Mr Furze.
Lawrence But you haven't — read this?
Alexandra Oh yes. I'm a great admirer of Mr Bernard Shaw.
Lawrence (*astonished*) Are you?
Alexandra I admire his politics. And his attitudes to women. I heard him
lecture once. Have you ever heard him lecture, Mr Furze?
Lawrence No. I would love to, but — no. I go to many lectures in the
evenings — if there is no admission charge. I very much wish to fill in the
s-s-substantial gaps in my education.
Alexandra Excellent. So which part are you taking in A Midsummer Night's
Dream?
Lawrence I was to have played Lys-s-sander.
Alexandra My lover.
Lawrence I beg your pardon?
Alexandra In the play. Didn't you hear? I am taking the part of Hermia.
Hermia is in love with Lysander.
Lawrence (*embarrassed*) Ah. Yes.
Alexandra You said you *were* to have played Lysander.
Lawrence Yes. I fear I cannot. I must leave. I think I am unsuited to amateur
dramatics.
Alexandra Why?
Lawrence Because of my s-s-s-s-s-s ——
Alexandra Your stammer?
Lawrence Yes. I had hoped I could overcome it. I have taken lessons at the
S-s-s-s-s-s-City College of Elocution, but as you s-s-s-s-s-s ——

Alexandra As I see. Yes, I see. But it will be different in a play. I think you could manage with lines of Shakespeare that you had already learned by rote.

Lawrence Perhaps.

Alexandra (*looking earnestly at Lawrence*) I would be very sorry if you did not take part in *A Midsummer Night's Dream*, Mr Furze.

Lawrence Well, I ... I ... (*Confused; abruptly changing the subject*) So, Miss De Lainey, what are your interests?

Alexandra Everything.

Lawrence Everything?

Alexandra Yes, everything in the whole wide world. There is so much out there — so many new and exciting things — and I want to know about all of them.

Lawrence (*slightly cynically*) When you say "new and exciting things", Miss De Lainey, do you mean musical comedies and Bridge and Ping-Pong?

Alexandra No, Mr Furze. I mean new and exciting ideas. And new and exciting science.

Lawrence Which is used to make rich men's toys like motor cars?

Alexandra The motor car is more than a toy, Mr Furze. It is the future. The purity of the future. Think how the streets of London smell with all ... (*She tries to put it delicately*) With what is left by the horses. The motor car offers a future of pure, unpolluted air. That is where science and invention are good — when they are harnessed to help the people, not just to pamper them.

Lawrence (*enthusiastically*) Oh, I agree. I agree so heartily with you. There is so much that can be done. So much good can come out of new inventions.

Alexandra And not just new ways of killing people.

Lawrence No. This is a new century, and this must be the century that puts paid to war once and for all. The war that has just ended — that must be the last there ever is.

Alexandra I agree.

Lawrence If enough people think as we do, we can ensure that that is what happens.

Alexandra It can happen. It will happen.

Lawrence And crime too. Crime can be eliminated.

Alexandra I'm not so sure about that.

Lawrence (*growing in confidence and in no danger of stammering*) It can. First it must become impossible for criminals to get away with their evil deeds.

Alexandra And how will that ever happen?

Lawrence It's closer than you might think, Miss De Lainey.

Alexandra Please call me Alexandra.

Lawrence (*surprised*) Alexandra?

Alexandra Yes, Lawrence.

Lawrence Very well. Have you heard of fingerprints, Alexandra?

Alexandra Only the ones my little sisters leave on Mama's best brocades.

Lawrence No. Fingerprints are the newest way to identify criminals. They mean that soon criminals will always be identifiable and so there will be no point in their committing crimes.

Alexandra I don't understand.

Lawrence Listen, there's a man I've met — a policeman called Charles Stockley Collins — dashed brainy fellow ... Well, he's in charge of what's called the Central Fingerprint Branch, and he organized an experiment on Derby Day.

Alexandra What, Derby Day just past?

Lawrence Yes, June the fourth, couple of weeks back. Anyway, Epsom Downs on Derby Day ... There are always all kinds of rogues and sharpers and tinkers up there — and fifty-four men were arrested by the police.

Alexandra For what?

Lawrence Doesn't matter. All kinds of crimes. But this is the point: Charles Stockley Collins took all their fingerprints.

Alexandra Took their fingerprints?

Lawrence Yes. You press the tips of the fingers in ink — it makes a mark. Anyway, that night after the Derby he checked all fifty-four of the sets of fingerprints with the records held at Scotland Yard, and twenty-nine of them matched up.

Alexandra What did that mean?

During the following speech, Harry Trunchpole, unseen by the two on stage, enters through the door US, *and listens to the conversation*

Lawrence It meant Charles Stockley Collins could prove that twenty-nine of the men had been guilty of other crimes before. So at the Petty Sessions the next morning, those twenty-nine received rather tougher sentences than they were expecting. I tell you, the fingerprinting system will completely destroy crime.

Alexandra Well, goodness me. And I thought Derby Day was just about horses.

Harry (*taking his cue and moving forward*) The horses are the most important part. Topping race this year. I was there, just along from the King's box. And everyone swore that Sceptre was going to do the business, because he'd already won both the Guineas — One Thousand and Two Thousand —— but I had a sneaking fancy for Bob Sievier's Ardpatrick. And didn't it romp home? Came in at a hundred to fourteen. Lucky for those of us who'd had a substantial wager on the nose.

Lawrence (*awkwardly*) Um ... Yes ... Well ...

Harry Good to see you again, Alex.

Alexandra And you, Harry.

Lawrence (*cast down*) You two know each other?

Harry You could say I'm a friend of the family. Oh, by the way, Mr Furze, Mr De Lainey's very keen for all the cast to have a look at the stage through there.

Lawrence Ah.

Harry Straight away, he said.

Lawrence S-S-S-S-S-S ——

Harry Straight away, yes.

Lawrence (*moving towards the door* UR) I'd better go, then.

Alexandra So, Mr Furze, you're not going to give up the part of Lysander? You're not going to leave?

Lawrence No. I'll s-s-s-s-s ——

Alexandra Stay.

Lawrence (*going out through the door*) Yes.

Lawrence exits

Harry You're looking dashed pretty, Alex.

Alexandra Harry, you know I am not partial to compliments.

Harry Frightfully sorry. Can't help it, though. Just speak as I find. It's in my nature.

Alexandra Well, it is not in my nature to enjoy a man making love to me.

Harry It'll come, Alexandra. Just a matter of time.

Alexandra's face registers she doesn't think this worthy of response

You know we talked about having an evening together ...

Alexandra You may have talked about it.

Harry Oh, I don't mean just the two of us, obviously. I'm not that kind of fellow. All be perfectly above board. A party of people. I'm not the chap to threaten a lady's reputation.

Alexandra I'm glad to hear it.

Harry So how about a bit of supper and a show one of these nights?

Alexandra I'm sorry, Harry. I have no taste for farces and musical comedies.

Harry Good Lord, no. I wasn't thinking of that kind of tommy-rot. Beerbohm Tree's *Merry Wives of Windsor's* just opened at His Majesty's.

Alexandra (*excitedly*) Oh yes. I read about it in *The Saturday Review*.

Harry Apparently, he makes his first entrance as Falstaff riding a real horse. Tickets a bit tricky to come by, but I've got some contacts.

Gus enters quietly from the door UR *and stands looking at Alexandra and Harry*

Alexandra You mean you could get tickets?

Harry Of course. Always helps to know the right people. Oh, Alex, say yes. Your father approves of my escorting you.

Alexandra Does he?

Harry Well, I haven't actually asked him yet, but I'm sure he will. You see, my father's got a title.

Alexandra But has he any money?

Harry Well ...

Alexandra My father is much more interested in money than titles, Harry.

Harry I'll win him round with my devilish charm, don't you worry. (*Taking her hand*) Come on, Alex. Just name a day for our little jaunt.

Alexandra Well, I ... (*She notices Gus and snatches her hand away*) You will excuse me. I must go and join my father.

Alexandra hurries off through the door UL

Gus (*advancing on Harry*) What game is this you're playing, Harry? You encouraged me to believe that I could train my sights on Miss De Lainey.

Harry Sorry, old fellow. Guilty of a slight deception there.

Gus Then why the deuce did you get me into this farrago?

Harry Mr De Lainey needed men for his production ...

Gus And so you got me in under false pretences, just so that you could ingratiate yourself with the old buffer?

Harry (*with a shrug*) You and Monty, yes.

Gus While you've been making doe-eyes at the eldest daughter all the time?

Harry nods

You unutterable bounder!

Harry Oh, don't get the hump, Gus. It's not as if the old cove hasn't got other daughters. There's Miss Arabella.

Gus I can't wait till she's old enough to be mashed, can I? And she ain't going to inherit as much as the first, is she?

Harry No.

Gus Huh. The Jews have already been damned sniffy about extending my credit for six months.

Harry Come off it, a man of your breeding can always borrow a bit more.

Gus That's all my eye, Harry. I'm really dished unless I can ——

Sydney De Lainey enters through the door UR, *with, through both doors, all the rest of the Bellingford Amateur Dramaticks' members in his wake*

Sydney De Lainey Um disappointed at the leck of electricity.

Mr Galley Mr De Lainey, this Institute was built for the Jubilee. That's fifteen years ago. Wasn't so much electricity around then.
Sydney De Lainey No. Never mind. Perhaps I will have the Institute convarted to electricity.
Mr Galley Oh, I don't think the council would like that.
Sydney De Lainey No matter. Thar is much else to done, me buy. Tame eneff for everything. Me production will still be a gret siccess.
Mrs Littlehouse Mr De Lainey, surely we're talking about my production. Or at least the Bellingford Amateur Dramaticks' production.
Sydney De Lainey Bah no mins, Messes Littlehoss. When Sydney De Lainey pots his resosses behind a play, it becomes a Sydney De Lainey production.
Mrs Littlehouse But ——
Sydney De Lainey Mr Galliah, me buy.
Mr Galley Yes, Guv'nor.
Sydney De Lainey Wud you show mia the dressing-rums?
Mr Galley We don't have dressing-rooms as such, Guv'nor. But I have made a very convenient system of framework and curtains, which converts some of the space in here into a dressing area. (*Proudly*) My own design and my own construction, you know.
Miss Horton (*appalled at the idea*) Are the ladies and the gentlemen expected to share the same dressing area?
Lydia Farrelly (*intrigued by the idea*) Oh, that could be a trifle interesting.
Monty I'll say!
Mr Galley No, no, ladies, of course not. My design incorporates a central dividing curtain. There will be no offence to anyone's proprieties, I can assure you.
Miss Horton I am very relieved to hear it.
Sydney De Lainey God. Mr Galliah, me buy.
Mr Galley Yes, Mr De Lainey.
Sydney De Lainey Go to me carrr.
Mr Galley To your car, yes.
Sydney De Lainey Spick to my chauffeur, Desborough. Ask him to give you the box from the luggage compartment. The contents are cuppies of *A Midsummer Nate's Drim*. I have hud them specially prunted for my production. Fetch them, Mr Galliah.
Mr Galley Very good, Guv'nor.

Mr Galley goes off through the exit DL

Branston Parrish But we've all got copies of the play.
Sydney De Lainey Nut of the vushen we will be performing.
Mrs Littlehouse You haven't dared to take liberties with Shakespeare's precious poetry, have you, Mr De Lainey?

Sydney De Lainey Teck liberties? No. I have marley med the play into something that will wuk on the stedge.

Branston Parrish And what changes does that involve?

Sydney De Lainey Only a few cuts and minor changes to some carcters.

Branston Parrish I hope you haven't touched my Bottom.

There are minor giggles from the rest of the cast; they're too anxious to laugh much

Sydney De Lainey I hev done only what is requard. And yar a vey fortunate feller. As Bottom, you will have the best ass's head ever sin on any stedge.

Branston Parrish Oh?

Sydney De Lainey I have made contect with the engineer who creates some of the must complicated stedge properties for Sir Henry Irving himself. He is creating — to mah own desarn — a magnificent ass's head. With ar-tic-u-lated ears.

Branston Parrish (*pleased at the prospect*) Oh. I should be able to work out some good comic business with that.

Sydney De Lainey In my productions, Mr Parrish, *I* wuk out ull the bus'ness, comic or otherwuz.

Branston Parrish Now listen here ——

Sydney De Lainey I will also be using Sir Henry Irving's armourer to create the swords for the show.

Monty Are there any swords in *A Midsummer Night's Dream*?

Sydney De Lainey (*firmly*) Yes. And mah own companiah — De Lainey Dimonds — wull be creating the crahns for the two Quins.

Miss Horton (*pleased*) What, so Hippolyta will have a real diamond crown?

Sydney De Lainey She wull indid. So will Ti-ta-ni-aaah.

Miss Horton How wonderful!

Sydney De Lainey And both putts will be pled by mah wuff, Mod.

Miss Horton (*appalled*) What?

Sydney De Lainey Then I will also ——

Miss Horton But Hippolyta is my part. You cannot just ——

Sydney De Lainey I wull do wut is nec-ess-ary to mek the play a siccess!

Miss Horton Oh! (*Coming over all faint*) Miss Sandwich, do you have any smelling salts?

Miss Sandwich Yes, of course, Miss Horton.

Miss Sandwich sits Miss Horton down and fusses around her

Sydney De Lainey (*ignoring them*) I will also be engedging an orchestraaah for our production — for the ballets, interludes, entr'actes and comic dances.

Monty Ballets, interludes, entr'actes and comic dances?

Sydney De Lainey Yes. The orchestraaah will be playing the music of Mendelssohn. Can you play the music of Mendelssohn, Miss Brabazon?

Miss Brabazon I can play anything I'm paid to play, Mr De Lainey. So long as it's not profane.

Sydney De Lainey Thus is must en-cour-ag-ing.

Mr Galley enters with a box of books

(*To Mr Galley*) Exsullent, Mr Galliah me buy. Give the cuppies rund.

Mr Galley passes the scripts round during the following

Mrs Littlehouse But, Mr De Lainey, I think I must make one thing clear. We are the Bellingford Amateur Dramaticks. This is a B.A.D. production. And though we are very grateful for any assistance you may give us, you can't just take it over.

Sydney De Lainey Messes Littlehoss, do you wish to tek advuntidge of the scenery and dresses I'm offering to peffor?

Mrs Littlehouse Yes, of course. But ——

Sydney De Lainey And the orchestraaah?

Mrs Littlehouse Well, yes.

Sydney De Lainey The dimond crahns? The swords? The ass's head? With ar-tic-u-lated ears?

Mrs Littlehouse As I said, we appreciate these things, but ——

Sydney De Lainey So you accept me generosity in one way. I think you shud also be gretful for the fect that I am prepared to tek on yah little play and turn it into a Sydney De Lainey production.

Mrs Littlehouse Yes, I'm very grateful, but ——

Sydney De Lainey (*ignoring her*) Yah ull huv cuppies? Thun sit ye dun.

They all sit

Lydia Farrelly (*moving close to Sydney De Lainey*) May I sit beside you, Mr De Lainey?

Sydney De Lainey (*slightly thrown to see her, but quickly recovering himself*) Of course, of course.

Lydia Farrelly sits beside Sydney De Lainey

Splundid. Let the ridding of *A Midsummer Nate's Drim* commence. (*He clears his throat as if to start reading*)

Gus   "Now, fair Hippolyta, our nuptial hour
              Draws on apace. Four happy days bring ——"

Sydney De Lainey silences Gus with heavy coughing

Sydney De Lainey Excyuzz me. Whut are you doin'?
Gus I was starting to read. Theseus opens the play. I'm playing Theseus.
Sydney De Lainey No, you're nut.
Gus What?
Sydney De Lainey I am plang Theseus.
Mrs Littlehouse But I thought you were playing Oberon.
Sydney De Lainey I am plang Theseus *and* Oberon. And, incidentlah, for
this evening's ridding of the plar, I will read all the putts myself.
Branston Parrish But why the devil should you do that?
Sydney De Lainey Otherwise what means will the rest of you have of
knowing how the demmed lines should be read?
           (*Reading*) "Nah, fair Hupp-o-lyta, ar nuptial arrr
              Droz on apess. Four huppy dez brung in
              Another moooon — but O, methinks, how slooooow ..."

The rest of the cast look on in gloomy disbelief

The Lights slowly go down

The CURTAIN *falls*

SCENE 2

The same. A week later, Tuesday the 24th of June. Late afternoon

*The only major change made in the Committee Room between the scenes is
the replacement of the picture of Queen Victoria with one of King Edward
VII. This is garlanded with red, white and blue ribbons, bunting which has
been put up in honour of the Coronation, due to take place two days later. And
the committee table has been removed, along with the box of Ping-Pong
equipment*

*Though some natural light comes in through the window, the gas-lights are
still needed*

*When the CURTAIN rises. Miss Brabazon is sitting at the piano. Maud De
Lainey is conducting a ballet rehearsal for the four fairies — Peaseblossom
(Arabella), Moth (Amelia), Cobweb (Alberta) and Mustardseed (Myrtle
Throckmorton). The four dancers are still, in their opening positions*

Maud Right. Let's just run it through. And I want your absolute best, girls. Imagine you are performing it for the King's Coronation on Thursday. In your own time, Miss Brabazon.

Miss Brabazon dourly thumps out the opening chords of Mendelssohn's "Wedding March", and the four start to dance. Though the three De Lainey girls are quite light on their feet and competent, Myrtle Throckmorton is far too large and clumsy ever to make a ballet dancer. She is constantly off the beat, making the wrong steps and waving her arms in gestures that are too elaborate. When, at the end of the short routine, the girls end in a tableau, she wobbles awkwardly, out of position

Still some work to do, I fear, ladies.

Her daughters look aggrieved

Though you three were all very good.

Her daughters simper at her

Myrtle ...

Myrtle Throckmorton Yes, Mrs De Lainey.

Maud You are rather larger than the other girls.

Myrtle Throckmorton I'm rather older than the other girls.

Maud Yes. I was not just referring to your size —though one is put to a difficulty trying to ignore it. What I was referring to was your largeness of gesture.

Myrtle Throckmorton I'd thought that Mustardseed was probably more flamboyant than the other fairies. You know, a more flamboyant character. I see her as the fairy who's a bit different from the others. She's the one with romantic ideas, who's really wanting to fall in love herself and is therefore a little jealous of Titania and Bottom.

Maud Do you, Miss Throckmorton? And is that surmise based on something said to you by Mr De Lainey?

Myrtle Throckmorton No, Mrs De Lainey.

Maud Then I would ask you to put all such thoughts from your mind. It is Mr De Lainey who decides what your character is like.

Myrtle Throckmorton (*put in her place*) Yes, Mrs De Lainey.

Maud Now I would like to try the dance through once again. And this time, Myrtle, smaller gestures please. Mustardseed is not a romantic. She is no different from any of the other fairies.

Amelia Except she's about twice the size.

Amelia's sisters giggle. Maud smiles. She finds it hard to get cross with her daughters

Maud Right, Miss Brabazon. If you would be so kind …

Miss Brabazon thumps out the opening chords, and the girls take up their opening positions, Myrtle Throckmorton looking extremely insecure

Sydney De Lainey makes an entrance through the door DL. *He is carrying nothing himself, but is followed by Mrs Littlehouse, laden down with boxes (a smart wooden one and a large cardboard one) and a couple of swords*

Maud Stop, Miss Brabazon! Mr De Lainey is arrived.

Miss Brabazon stops playing. The girls stay in their positions. Myrtle Throckmorton wobbles dangerously. Mrs Littlehouse places her burden down on the floor

Sydney De Lainey Ah, my lev. Do not stop for me. Ah shud lev to see mah gels perform. Ah shud lev to see the Dance of the Ferries.
Maud Very well, Miss Brabazon. In your own time …

Miss Brabazon once again starts to play the "Wedding March". The girls dance. The De Lainey girls are once again well-drilled and competent, but Myrtle Throckmorton is so inhibited by her audience, and by trying to concentrate on making her gestures smaller, that she is even worse than before

Sydney De Lainey (*before they have finished*) Step! Step! This will not do by any mins.

The dancing stops untidily. So does Miss Brabazon. The De Lainey daughters gather together smugly, isolating Myrtle Throckmorton

Marm, which putt are you plang?
Myrtle Throckmorton I'm playing Mustardseed.
Sydney De Lainey No longer! (*Pointing off* R *with a dramatic gesture*) You are nut god enough to tek putt in a Sydney De Lainey production.
Myrtle Throckmorton What? But Mustardseed's my first speaking part. I've been looking forward to this so much. I … Oh … (*She is overcome by tears*)

Myrtle Throckmorton rushes off, wailing, through the door DR

Mrs Littlehouse Mr De Lainey! Now you've upset her.
Sydney De Lainey Ah hud no choice. Mah art demanded she should go.

Mrs Littlehouse (*following Myrtle*) It'll take ages to calm her down.

Mrs Littlehouse exits

Sydney De Lainey God-afternoon, dutters.
Daughters Good-afternoon, Papa.
Sydney De Lainey Is there anything you nid, my little enjels?
Amelia We need a new Mustardseed.
Sydney De Lainey Thet is true. And mebbee you also nid some ace crims and Carnation bon-bons ...?
Daughters Ooh, yes!
Maud So where are we going to find a new Mustardseed?
Sydney De Lainey Nerrer in saize to our gels.
Alberta Papa, there's my friend Daisy.
Sydney De Lainey Dezzy? Dezzy?
Maud Daughter of the banker. Mr Winsom. Muswell Hill.
Sydney De Lainey (*impressed*) Oh yes, indeed.
Alberta The one who keeps rabbits.
Sydney De Lainey The benker keeps rebbits?
Alberta No, Papa. Daisy keeps rabbits. And she's a good dancer, isn't she, Mama?
Maud Excellent, Alberta.
Alberta Papa, may we go and ask Daisy to join us? It would be such fun.
Sydney De Lainey Yes. My enjels. Tell Desborough to teck you.
Alberta (*clapping her hands*) Ooh, in the car, good!
Amelia (*running for the exit*) I'm going to sit in Papa's seat!
Sydney De Lainey (*calling after them*) And bay yourselves some ace crims and Carnation bon-bons on the way.

Amelia and Alberta rush out

Maud looks at her husband and then at Miss Brabazon

Miss Brabazon (*sitting firmly in her seat with her arms folded*) I was to be paid till six o'clock.
Maud Don't worry. You'll still be paid.
Miss Brabazon (*getting up sharply and hurrying* DR) Oh, that's all right then.

Miss Brabazon exits DR

Maud looks piercingly at her husband

Sydney De Lainey Whut?

Still she stares at him

Whut is it, Mod?

Maud That Miss Farrelly ... Lydia Farrelly, who's playing Helena ... you know her from somewhere.

Sydney De Lainey I think, my lev, you are mistekken.

Maud I'm not. (*Her middle-class accent slipping into Cockney*) I can always tell when you are up to something.

Sydney De Lainey I am not, my lev.

Maud Yes, you are, and when I have proof, it'll be the Divorce Court, Sydney.

Sydney De Lainey (*suddenly losing his accent and speaking in vicious Cockney*) You'd never dare, Maud! Divorce? Your reputation'd be ruined as well as mine.

Maud Oh, I'd dare, Sydney. And there's nothing you could do to stop me!

Sydney De Lainey Nothing?

There is an impasse as the two Cockneys stare at each other

(*Resuming his Henry Irving accent*) "Nothing wull come of nothing." (*He picks up the smart wooden box Mrs Littlehouse brought in*) I think I met have something hiah that met restore your feth in me, me lev.

Maud (*back in her middle-class accent; intrigued*) Oh?

Sydney De Lainey opens the box, revealing two blue-baize-lined compartments, in each of which is a different diamond tiara

Sydney De Lainey (*holding the tiaras up in turn*) The crown of Ti-ta-niaaah ... and the crown of Hi-ppo-ly-taaah!

Maud (*greedily impressed*) Oh, Sydney! (*She takes one tiara and puts it on her head*)

Sydney De Lainey Both of which crowns wull, after the production, be the crowns of — Mrs Mod De Lainey.

Maud (*trying on the other tiara*) Sydney ... they're beautiful.

Sydney De Lainey Yes. The farnest African dimonds, cut by the farnest English craftsman.

Maud (*holding the two tiaras in front of her and looking at them greedily*) Beautiful ... beautiful ...

Sydney De Lainey Now whut were we tokking about?

Maud (*coming to kiss him on the cheek*) Do you know, Sydney, I can't remember.

Sydney De Lainey (*smiling with satisfaction*) God. (*Moving towards the door* UR) I must fend Mr Galliah. I nid his curtains set up, if we are to hev costumes tred on tonate. Pot the crahns away, Mod — and do not let them out of your sate.

Maud (*setting to work to put the crowns away; calling after Sydney De Lainey*) No, of course not, Sydney.

Sydney De Lainey exits

Harry, Monty and Gus enter from the lobby. Branston Parrish, holding a different copy of the text from the one he was given in Scene 1, comes in a little way behind them

Harry (*to Gus and Monty*) ... it's a dashed funny musical comedy and it features some of the prettiest girls I've ever seen.

Gus So did you go backstage?

Monty Were you a "Stage Door Johnny"? Did you actually get to see some of the girls in their drawers?

Harry (*slyly*) Well, maybe I did just ... (*He sees the crowns that Maud is putting away and whistles*) Now those are dashed convincing. Nice bit of paste there.

Maud I can assure you these are not paste. They are the genuine article.

Harry Are they, by Jove?

Maud (*haughtily*) Sydney De Lainey never deals in paste.

Branston Parrish Is your husband about, Mrs De Lainey? I need to have a word with him.

Maud Here he is.

Sydney De Lainey enters from the door UR, *followed by Mr Galley. Maud picks up the closed box and goes out through the door* UL

Sydney De Lainey You wish a wud with me, Mr Purrish?

Branston Parrish Yes, I ——

Sydney De Lainey One mumment. Mr Galley wull nid some help putting up his curtain arrangements. You young men cun assist him.

Gus Just a minute. We're not deuced navvies, you know.

Harry Oh, come on, Gus. We can do it. No skin off our nose.

Monty Be a bit of a lark. My mater says manual labour can be a lot of fun.

Gus How would she know?

Harry Yes, of course we'll do it. Mr Galley, show us what's required.

Monty And we'll buckle down to it with vim.

Mr Galley (*leading the way through the door* DR) If you like to follow me, gentlemen. I made the construction so that it folds down very neatly into a conveniently small space ...

Mr Galley exits, followed by Harry, Monty and Gus

Sydney De Lainey You hed something to sigh, Mr. Purrish.

Branston Parrish Yes. Mr De Lainey, I cannot tolerate the way you have made cuts to Shakespeare's fine play of *A Midsummer Night's Dream.*

Sydney De Lainey Ah hev med the cuts so that the play will wuk on stedge.

Branston Parrish But you have cut the part of Bottom down until he becomes a mere supernumerary in the action.

Sydney De Lainey I have marely followed the admirable exumple of Sir Henry Irving.

Branston Parrish No, you have not. Henry Irving never acted in *A Midsummer Night's Dream* and do you know why? Because he recognized there wasn't a part for him. There is no one central role in the play, so he couldn't shine as he wished to.

Sydney De Lainey I know. It was ah thought of the clever device of playing both O-ber-on and The-se-us.

Branston Parrish (*opening his book*) But in the introduction to Sir Henry Irving's own edition of the play we read: (*reading*) "We must hold that Nick Bottom is the gem of this work. No more masterly portrait of good-humoured self–conceit has ever been drawn than ——"

Sydney De Lainey (*interrupting*) Mr Purrish, may ah remand you thet in the General Introduction to the sem set of volumes, Sir Henry also writes, "The vushen presented was strictly the original text without in-ter-pol-a-tions, but simply such omissions and trans-po-sitions as have been fund essential for dra-ma-tic rep-res-en-tation."

Branston Parrish (*waving his book*) But his printed version of the *Dream* doesn't butcher the text as you have done!

Sydney De Lainey I am nut a demmed butcher!

Branston Parrish (*picking up one of the prop swords Mrs Littlehouse brought in; furiously*) Yes, you damned well are – and if you don't change the way you're doing things you're likely *be* butchered!

Sydney De Lainey (*suddenly changing the subject*) Mr Purrish, would you like to see your ass's head?

Branston Parrish (*the wind taken out of his sails*) What?

Sydney De Lainey (*opening the large cardboard box that Mrs Littlehouse brought in*) With ar-tic-u-lated ears.

Branston Parrish (*his anger defused*) Oh. Well ... (*Putting the sword back down again*) Yes, I would be interested.

Sydney De Lainey (*dramatically bringing the ass's head out of the box*) Behold!

The ass's head is indeed a magnificent creation. And it does have articulated ears, which can be manipulated by strings dangling down from the neck. Though the wearer's face cannot be seen, there is a gauze piece through which he can speak. Branston Parrish is very impressed by what he sees

(*Handing the head across*) Tray it, Mr Purrish.

Branston Parrish (*tickled to death with it*) I most certainly will. (*He puts the ass's head on and starts clowning about. He brays*)

Miss Horton and Miss Sandwich enter from the lobby and stand watching the scene

Sydney De Lainey Tray the strings, Mr Purrish. To ar-tic-u-late the ears.

Branston Parrish does so. The ears flick up and down. Unaware of the arrival of the women, Branston Parrish brays and starts doing a little jig. He stops

Miss Horton It seems that you have found your intellectual level at last, Mr Parrish.

Miss Sandwich giggles

Branston Parrish (*taking the head off and looking slyly at Miss Horton*) At least when I wish to look like an ass, Miss Horton, I require artificial assistance. Whereas in your case nature has done it for you.

Miss Sandwich giggles again. Miss Horton quells her with a look

Miss Horton Mr De Lainey, is it true that you wish us to try on our dresses this evening?

Sydney De Lainey Yes.

Miss Horton It seems extremely early in rehearsals for such an undertaking.

Sydney De Lainey May wuff is in charge of the costumes. Mod has them here on epproval from the hiring companiah. We must reserve whut we nid for November.

Miss Horton Oh, very well.

Branston Parrish (*with mock politeness*) And do remind me, Miss Horton, which costume it is that you will be trying on? Which part is it you are playing now?

Miss Horton (*through tight lips*) Peter Quince.

Branston Parrish How appropriate. Such a sour fruit, the quince, isn't it?

Miss Horton bridles

Of course, when I was young, we loved to go to the theatre to see ladies in "breeches parts". (*He chuckles fruitily*) Only chance we young blades got to see a nice pair of female legs.

Miss Horton I can assure you, Mr Parrish, that my legs will not be on display.

Branston Parrish No. The Lord is very merciful, isn't he?

Miss Sandwich giggles again

Miss Horton I don't know what you're laughing at, Miss Sandwich.
Miss Sandwich Well, it was rather amusing.
Miss Horton Don't forget. You're going to be dressed as a man too.
Miss Sandwich Oh yes. (*Crestfallen*) Oh dear.
Sydney De Lainey The costumes are led out in the Holl, if you wud care to inspect 'em.
Miss Horton (*gloomily*) Oh, I suppose we'd better find out the worst. Come along, Miss Sandwich.

Miss Horton and Miss Sandwich exit UR

Mr Galley enters DR, *leading in Harry, Monty and Gus. They are all carrying parts of Mr Galley's dressing-room structure. Mr Galley and Harry bring on one of the outer panels, Gus and Monty carry the other. They fix these in position during the ensuing dialogue*

Branston Parrish (*putting the ass's head on; to the approaching young men*) Hey, feast your eyes on this! Tell me what you think of my ass's head?
Harry What ass's head? Have you got one on?
Branston Parrish What a wag you are, you young shaver. (*He heads towards the door* UR) I must see what I look like. There's a mirror in the foyer.

Branston exits, braying delightedly

Sydney De Lainey Ah must check the dresses we are to see.
Mr Galley All laid out in the hall, Mr De Lainey, like you asked.
Sydney De Lainey (*heading for the door* UL) Exsullent, Mr Galliah.

Sydney De Lainey exits

Mr Galley Right, young gentlemen ... (*To Harry and Gus*) If you two can fix these panels to the brackets there on the wall — (*to Monty*) you can come and help me get the middle panel. (*He heads for the door* DR)
Monty (*following Mr Galley*) Is that the one between the ladies' and the gentlemen's dressing areas?
Mr Galley Yes.
Monty (*giggling*) And has it got a peephole in it — a chink like the Wall in *Pyramus and Thisbe* — so we chaps can look through and see the ladies in their drawers?

Mr Galley and Monty exit

Mr Galley (*off*) No, it most certainly hasn't!

Harry and Gus fix the two outer panels in position during the ensuing dialogue

Gus (*after checking that they're alone in the room*) So, Harry, how's your courtship of the lovely Miss De Lainey going?
Harry None so dusty — though there are a couple of small insects in the honey.
Gus Oh?
Harry Well, her papa seems rather distrustful of my intentions ...
Gus Not as much of a fool as he looks, is he?
Harry Hm. And then there's Lys-s-s-s-sander ...
Gus Taken a shine to young Mr Furze, has she?
Harry Yes. Of course, he's even more of a non-starter than I am so far as her old man's concerned, but she seems to be spoons on him — which is damned inconvenient.
Gus So are you going to give up the chase?
Harry Don't you believe it.

Mr Galley and Monty enter, carrying the central panel

I have a little plan which —— (*He sees Mr Galley and Monty and stops*)
Mr Galley Here we are. There's a bracket for this one on the wall, and all.
Monty Is that me done and dusted?
Mr Galley No, Mr Pottle. (*He indicates the door* DL) You go back there for the cross-strut, and I'll get the front curtains, which are kept over here.

Mr Galley exits DR

Monty (*moving towards the door* DL) Oh, very well. Deuced slave-driver, he is.
Harry (*calling after Monty*) I thought your mater says manual labour can be a lot of fun.
Monty (*as he goes through the door*) Yes, but dash it, moderation in all things.

Monty exits

During the ensuing dialogue, Harry and Gus put up the central dividing panel

Gus (*when he's once again sure they're alone*) So what is your plan, Harry?
   For the lovely Alexandra?
Harry She's agreed to spend an evening with me.
Gus The devil she has.
Harry Oh, all right and proper. Big party of us going to see Shakespeare.
Gus Shakespeare? Not your usual speed.
Harry *Merry Wives of Windsor*. Beerbohm Tree at His Majesty's. On
   Thursday.
Gus Coronation night.
Harry Exactly.
Gus So where are you really taking her?
Harry Light supper before the show. In a restaurant where — remarkably —
   the rest of my large party won't have showed up.
Gus Where is it, you rogue?
Harry Romano's in the Strand.

Gus lets out a low whistle

   If it was good enough for our king when he was just Dirty Bertie — with
   Lily Langtry and the others ...
Gus Indeed. And you've booked one of the upstairs rooms, I assume?
Harry Oh yes. So King Edward won't be the only one whose endeavours get
   crowned that night.

Gus chuckles

   Which means I will have in my hands Miss De Lainey's precious
   reputation ...
Gus Amongst other even more precious portions of her.
Harry (*chuckling*) And when I tell this to her papa, and explain how it could
   all become very public indeed — the waiters at Romano's can be dashed
   indiscreet when you pay them to ... Well, under those circumstances, I
   don't think Mr De Lainey would stand in the way of our marriage.
Gus You're a cunning fox, Harry. I only wish my problems could be sorted
   out as easily.
Harry Well, I ——

*Monty enters carrying the cross-strut which goes across the top of the
dressing-room frame, locking the three panels in place*

   Ssh.
Monty I say, I had the very deuce of an idea while I was out there.
Harry Did you? Come on, let's get this up.

They line up the cross-strut during the following

Gus Going to have to stand on chairs, aren't we?

They move chairs into position and fix the cross-strut

Monty But I've had this spanking good idea.
Harry Arrange this in position first, then you tell us. Is it locked your end,
   Gus?
Gus Just needs a little ...

The cross-strut is fixed in place

   Ah ... there we are.
Harry There's mine fixed too. Good. Make damned fine navvies, we would.
   Let's just put some chairs out for people to lay out their costumes, eh?

They put a couple of chairs in each compartment during the following

Monty Can I tell you my idea now?
Harry Fire away, Monty.
Monty Well, look. (*Taking a pair of scissors out of his pocket*) I found these
   lying on a shelf out there. And look what I'm going to do with them. (*He
   goes boldly to the middle panel and cuts a slit in the curtain*) See!
Gus For heaven's sake, you blitherer!
Harry Stop playing the goat, Monty. What's that for?
Monty It's — (*he sniggers at his own daring*) so that we can look through
   and see the ladies in their drawers.
Harry You pathetic chump.
Monty What do you mean? Don't you want to see ladies in their drawers?

Gus and Harry look pityingly at Monty

   You mean you have already seen ladies in their drawers?
Gus And out of them, Monty.
Monty (*very impressed*) Crikey! You are quite the lads, aren't you?
Harry (*heading towards the door* DL) Come on, I need a smoke. Anyone else
   for a coffin-nail?
Gus (*following him*) I could do with one.
Monty (*following Gus; in an excited whisper*) Gus, could you actually tell
   me what ladies look like without their drawers on?

Mr Galley enters from the door DR, *carrying the pair of curtains that fit
across the front of the two changing compartments. He fixes the curtains
on the hooks, singing to himself G.W. Hunt's song, "Up in a Balloon",
starting by half-humming the chorus, and then going into a more robust*

performance. As he finishes the song, he finishes hooking up the curtains, closes them with a flourish, and looks up with satisfaction at his achievement

Mr Galley (*singing*) Up in a balloon, up in a balloon,
All among the little stars sailing round the moon,
Up in a balloon, up in a balloon,
It's something awfully jolly to be up in a balloon.

Next a comet went by 'midst fire like hail,
To give me a lift, I seized hold of his tail,
To where he was going I didn't enquire,
We'd gone past the moon till we couldn't get higher;
Yes, we'd got to the furthermost! Don't think I joke
When somehow I felt a great shock, I awoke!
When instead of balloon, moon and planets, I saw,
I'd tumbled from off my bed to the floor.

And there was no balloon — no balloon,
There were not any planets, and there wasn't any moon,
So never sup too heavy or by jingo very soon,
You're like to fancy you are going up in a balloon.

Mr Galley exits through the door DR

Alexandra and Lawrence enter through the door DL

Alexandra I don't think I've ever seen the streets so full.
Lawrence And with people of so many countries and colours. The Coronation will be a splendid day.
Alexandra Yes.
Lawrence I was wondering ——
Alexandra Hm?
Lawrence — whether we might be able to meet in the evening? There's a lecture on Ibsen at the Dialectical Society.
Alexandra (*enthusiastically*) Oh, that sounds wonderful! (*Remembering*) No. I can't. Not on Thursday.
Lawrence Are you really telling me that your father won't let you go out with me?
Alexandra No, I am not. I will go out with whom I please. But the day after tomorrow, I have a prior engagement.
Lawrence (*glumly*) Oh. It's no good, is it, Alexandra?
Alexandra What's no good.
Lawrence You and me.

Alexandra Of course it's good, Lawrence. It's the best thing that's ever happened in my life.

Lawrence And in mine. But we have no future together.

Alexandra Why ever not?

Lawrence Because you're rich. You're the daughter of Sydney De Lainey, the diamond merchant. And I'm just one of his accounts clerks.

Alexandra But, Lawrence, that couldn't matter less.

Lawrence Oh no?

Alexandra What have we been talking about all afternoon in the park? Socialism, Socialism, Socialism. Divisions of wealth and class don't matter.

Lawrence I think they suddenly do when it comes to the important things.

Alexandra What important things?

Lawrence Like marriage.

Alexandra Marriage? Lawrence, are you asking me to marry you?

Lawrence I would if there was any purpose to it. But there ain't.

Alexandra What do you mean?

Lawrence Your father would never agree to your marrying someone like me.

Alexandra Then who cares what my father thinks?

Lawrence (*a bit shocked by this*) What?

Alexandra And who cares about marriage?

Lawrence (*even more shocked*) I beg your pardon?

Alexandra If two people want to spend their lives together, who's to stop them?

Lawrence (*really quite alarmed now*) Without the blessing of the church?

Alexandra If necessary, yes. I love you, Lawrence …

Lawrence (*shaken*) Oh.

Alexandra And I'm going to be with you, married or not married.

Lawrence (*appalled*) You can't say that!

Alexandra Why not?

Lawrence Alexandra, are you telling me you believe in Free Love?

Alexandra Yes.

Lawrence But that's an terrible thing to say! I thought you were a nice innocent girl. I didn't realize you had thoughts like that!

Alexandra (*moving forward to kiss Lawrence*) Lawrence. Don't agitate yourself.

Alexandra kisses Lawrence on the lips. He leaps away, as if he's received an electric shock

Harry wanders in through the door DR. *He watches Alexandra and Lawrence during the following, but they are too caught up in their row to notice him*

Lawrence (*wiping his lips, disgusted*) You can't — kiss me! It is not natural for a woman to want to kiss a man! Oh, Alexandra, I thought we had so much. I did not realize you were that kind of girl!

Lawrence rushes off through the door DL, *in a terrible state*

Alexandra burst into tears

Harry What an odd cove.

Alexandra becomes aware of Harry and turns to face him, still crying

Most chaps spend their lives hoping their beloved is that kind of girl.
Alexandra (*sobbing*) Harry …
Harry (*moving chivalrously to take her in his arms*) Oh, look, come on, my angel. We can't have that lovely face spoiled with tears. (*Reaching into his pocket for a handkerchief*) Let's mop 'em up, shall we?
Alexandra Harry, you're so kind to me.
Harry (*smoothly*) Yes, I am, aren't I?
Alexandra Do *you* believe in Free Love?
Harry Oh, I think, in the right circumstances, between the right people — deuced good thing.
Alexandra And what about Socialism?
Harry (*evasively*) I'm sure there's a place for that too … somewhere in the scheme of things.

Lydia Farrelly enters through the door DL, *and looks on cynically at the scene that's being played out in front of her*

Harry Did that little tagrag of an accounts clerk get a bit fresh with you, Alex?
Alexandra No. Rather the reverse.
Harry (*puzzledly*) Oh. (*Changing the subject*) Must say I'm looking forward to Thursday evening.
Alexandra What? Oh yes, our — *Merry Wives of Windsor.*
Harry Mm.
Alexandra I'll read the play again before then.
Harry Good thinking.
Alexandra Will you too?
Harry (*who wouldn't in a thousand years*) What? Oh yes. Better had, hadn't I?
Alexandra Am I likely to know any of the others?
Harry Others?
Alexandra Of your large party at His Majesty's?

Harry Ah. Probably not. But I still think you'll have a splendid evening.

Harry, rather enjoying having Alexandra in his arms, moves his hands to hold her tighter. She looks up at him. They could almost be about to kiss ...

Lydia Farrelly pointedly clears her throat

Alexandra springs away from Harry's arms

Harry Didn't see you there.
Lydia Farrelly I'd never have guessed.
Alexandra (*embarrassedly*) I'm sorry ... I must ... Excuse me.

Alexandra hurries off through the door UL, *in confusion*

Lydia Farrelly So ... Is she ... (*Singing softly, to the tune of "The Boy I Love Is Up in the Gallery"*) "The girl you love ..."?
Harry (*singing softly*) "She's up in the gallery."
Lydia Farrelly I've seen you at Romano's, haven't I?
Harry Have you?
Lydia Farrelly Oh yes. You and a few more gentlemen not using their own names.
Harry Doesn't a fellow deserve a little fun now and then?
Lydia Farrelly I've never been against a bit of fun.
Harry (*drawing close to Lydia Farrelly as if about to kiss her*) Now that's what a chap likes to hear.
Lydia Farrelly So you want to catch Miss De Lainey, do you?
Harry (*drawing back*) Why not? Pretty little thing, ain't she?
Lydia Farrelly Certainly. And pretty well-cushioned financially.
Harry A chap has to maintain his manner of living somehow. And, sadly, I don't know any rich Americans.
Lydia Farrelly Mm. Of course, Mr De Lainey might not approve ...
Harry Well ...
Lydia Farrelly Think you a bit flighty and unreliable and — not rich enough for his precious daughter.
Harry Have to admit that's possible, yes. May be a bit of an ass in his acting, but when it comes to money, nobody gets anything past him.
Lydia Farrelly I could make him agree to anything you want ...
Harry Could you, by Jove?
Lydia Farrelly For a consideration.
Harry For a consideration, of course.
Lydia Farrelly A poor girl has to make a living somehow.
Harry If you can make Sydney De Lainey agree to my marrying Alexandra, I'll set you up for life.

Lydia Farrelly In a Mayfair apartment?
Harry Oh yes.
Lydia Farrelly With a maid?
Harry You drive a hard bargain. But yes, your own maid. In your own Mayfair apartment. (*He chuckles*) Where, after the wedding ... I might maybe come and pay the occasional call on you ...?
Lydia Farrelly (*with a little mock-curtsy*) I'll instruct my maid that I'm always in for Mr Harry Trunchpole.

They chuckle in complicity

Harry So, Lydia, what's the hold you have over old De Lainey?
Lydia Farrelly A very simple one. I have seen ——

The sound of Sydney De Lainey approaching the door UR *can be heard*

Sh!

Sydney De Lainey enters UR

Sydney De Lainey Rart! We must get on. Cud you summon one and allll beck here, Miss Farrelly?
Harry It's all right. I'll get 'em.

Harry hurries off through the door DR, *with a wink to Lydia Farrelly*

Sydney De Lainey (*trying to avoid Lydia Farrelly's eye; awkwardly*) I never fully billiv in a plar until I have sin the costumes.
Lydia Farrelly Don't you — Mr MacGregor?
Sydney De Lainey (*trying to bluff his way out*) Um sorry. I dunt know whut you min.
Lydia Farrelly Well, you do look remarkably like the Mr McGregor — who's such a regular at Romano's in the Strand — and who's such a very close and generous patron to my friend Nellie ...

Maud enters through the door UR, *unseen by Sydney De Lainey and Lydia Farrelly*

Sydney De Lainey leaps forward, grabs Lydia Farrelly's wrist, and thrusts his face close to hers

Sydney De Lainey (*in his threatening Cockney accent*) Don't you ever dare breathe a word of that to anyone! I'll kill you if I ... (*He becomes aware* *of Maud's presence, releases Lydia Farrelly's hand and attempts a cover-up, back in his Henry Irving voice)* Und thut, Miss Farrelly, is the kind of in-ten-si-tiah ah require you, as Helenah, to pot into your arguments with Hermiah.

Lydia Farrelly *(playing along)* I'll do my best, Mr De Lainey.

There is challenging and unforgiving eye contact between Sydney De Lainey and his wife for a moment, then he moves dramatically to the door UL and calls through into the hall

Sydney De Lainey Come one, come allll! You are requard in the Grin Rum!

The other cast members enter in dribs and drabs, some talking to each other. From DR come Harry, Myrtle Throckmorton, Mrs Littlehouse, Miss Brabazon and Mr Galley. From UR come Miss Horton and Miss Sandwich. From DL come Gus and Monty. And from UL come Branston Parrish (minus his ass's head) and Alexandra

Sydney De Lainey Rart. Messes Littlehoss, Miss Thruckmorton, fetch the dresses from the holl.

Mrs Littlehouse *(trying to be assertive)* Look, we're not your slaveys.

Sydney De Lainey Fetch the dresses!

Mrs Littlehouse *(failing to be assertive)* Oh, very well.

Mrs Littlehouse and Myrtle Throckmorton trail towards the door UR

Sydney De Lainey *(calling after them)* Bring them through the central dars! *(Pointing to the right-hand curtained section)* Gentlemen's costumes in this section. *(Pointing to the left-hand section)* Leddies' costumes this side.

Mrs Littlehouse and Myrtle Throckmorton nod dispiritedly and exit through the door UR

Sydney De Lainey Rart, now who shall we hev to tray on the costumes farst? Mr Pottle, let us see you in the garb of Puck.

Monty Oh righty-ho. Wonder what kind of toggery Puck'll wear? What larks, eh? I do, Mr De Lainey, incidentally know a lot of the lines already. My mater's been hearing me on them. She says I'm a deuced quick study.

Sydney De Lainey Exsullent! And let us see some of the leddies changing into thar costumes too.

Monty *(rather too enthusiastically, thinking of his peephole)* Oh yes, let's!

Sydney De Lainey Let us see our Payter Quince and Float the Bellers-mendah.

Miss Horton Oh dear.

Miss Sandwich Do we have to?

Monty (*disappointedly*) Yes, do we have to?

Sydney De Lainey Yes, indid. Go through to your tarring-harses, and we will hev a costume parade as soon as you are reddiah.

The central doors at the back of the stage are seen to open; unseen, Mrs Littlehouse and Myrtle Throckmorton enter and lay out the costumes from the hall during the following, then exit. The doors are not closed after they have finished

Miss Horton and Miss Sandwich go into the L compartment without enthusiasm and draw the curtains firmly after them. Monty goes into the R compartment. During the following they change into their costumes

Let us meck some space, so that we can see the actors in their fahnery. Mr Galliah, me buy, cud you teck the swords through to the holl?

Mr Galley (*picking up the swords and going out through the door* UL) Of course, Guv'nor.

Sydney De Lainey And now we must ——

Arabella, Amelia and Alberta, together with Daisy Winsom enter DL. Daisy, another rich man's overdressed daughter, is the same age as Alberta. She carries a wicker animal basket

Alberta Hallo, Papa.

Sydney De Lainey Ulberta, my enjel.

Alberta This is Daisy Winsom.

Daisy (*who can't pronounce her Rs*) It's a weal pleasure to meet you, Mr De Lainey.

Myrtle Throckmorton and Mrs Littlehouse come in through the door UL, and hear the next bit of dialogue. They are followed by Mr Galley

Sydney De Lainey God-evening, Daisy.

Amelia (*to the assembled throng*) Daisy's our new Mustardseed.

Sydney De Lainey Who must be bettah than the gret galumphing gel who was plang the putt.

Myrtle Throckmorton looks as if she might be about to cry again. Mrs Littlehouse takes her hand to comfort her

Daisy I've bwought Wedvers with me, Mr De Lainey.

Sydney De Lainey Wedvers?

Daisy Named after Sir Wedvers Butler, who led our bwave boys in the Boer War and waised the Siege of Ladysmith.

Sydney De Lainey Oh. And whut is Wedvers?

Daisy (*indicating the basket*) He's my very own wabbit. And he'd weally like to have a part in *A Midsummer Night's Dweam* too.

Sydney De Lainey (*uncertain*) Hm ...

Daisy Mr Beerbohm Twee has weal wabbits in his pwoductions.

Harry (*looking across at Alexandra*) And a real horse in his *Merry Wives of Windsor*.

Sydney De Lainey Then Mr Sydney De Lainey shall also have rill rebbits in his *Midsummer Nate's Drim*. An exsutlent thut. Do you have other rebbits, Daisy?

Daisy We have lots of wabbits, Mr De Lainey.

Sydney De Lainey (*with a lavish gesture*) Then tell them they will all have putts in my production! Messes Littlehoss.

Mrs Littlehouse Yes, Mr De Lainey?

Sydney De Lainey Will you see how our Quince and Float are procidding in the tarring-harse?

Mrs Littlehouse Yes, Mr De Lainey.

Mrs Littlehouse slips into the left-hand compartment, being very careful only to open the curtain the minimum, so that no-one can see inside

Sydney De Lainey Lut them show themselves when they are reddiah.

Mrs Littlehouse (*out of sight behind the curtain*) They're ready.

Miss Horton (*out of sight behind the curtain; in a fierce whisper*) No, we aren't!

Miss Sandwich (*out of sight behind the curtain, also in fierce whisper*) Certainly not!

Sydney De Lainey I wull give you the cue to drar the curtin, Messes Littlehoss.

Miss Horton (*out of sight behind the curtain, in a fierce whisper*) No!

Miss Sandwich (*out of sight behind the curtain, also in a fierce whisper*) Please!

Sydney De Lainey Reddiah, Messes Littlehoss. "Whut hempen homespuns hev we swaggerin' hiah?"

Mrs Littlehouse draws back the curtain. Miss Horton and Miss Sandwich are revealed, cowering and embarrassed in their costumes, which consist of the Victorians' idea of Athenian tunics and floppy straw hats. The tunics come to just above their knees, but each lady is still wearing her skirt underneath. Harry, Gus and Branston Parrish cannot restrain their laughter

Branston Parrish Dash it, Miss Horton, I knew if you searched long enough, you'd find a fashion that made you look attractive.
Maud Ladies, the costumes are not designed to be worn with skirts. Athenian peasant women did not wear skirts.
Miss Horton (*fiercely*) Well, these Athenian peasant women are going to wear skirts! Or they won't be in the production!
Maud Oh.

Monty totters against the curtain on the male side of the dressing-room, trying to get one of his boots on. The structure ripples and bulges. Monty falls out of the dressing-room, just managing to stay on his feet and still pulling on the recalcitrant boot. He is dressed in a costume mid-way between an Arthur Rackham fairy and Peter Pan, with red tights, a little red pointy cap on his head and red pointy boots. He looks a complete prat

Monty I can't get this dashed pixie boot on. Could one of you fellows give me a hand.?
Gus I'll do it, you prize ass.

Gus and Monty manage to get the boot on

Monty (*striking a pose*) There! What d'ye think?
Harry If that's what a spirit looks like, I'll stick to brandy.
Sydney De Lainey (*looking at Monty admiringly*) Exsullent, me buy, exsullent. Thus is a Pock worthy of my O-be-ron. (*He goes into acting mode, with elaborate gestures*)
"Fitch me tha harb and be thou hiah agaaain
Eaaaah the Lev-i-a-than cun swim a leeeeeg."
Monty (*doing exactly the same acting style as Sydney, also with elaborate gestures*)
"Ull pot a gardle rahnd abaht tha arth
In farty munnits!"
Harry (*laughing*) Is that how you're actually going to do it, Monty?
Monty Oh yes.
Sydney De Lainey (*again admiringly*) Splendid, me buy, splendid. You are a true *actor*! (*Rubbing his hands together with pleasure*) Now let us see some marr costumes. Mod, come with me to the holl. Who else wud like to see whut they'll be wahring? Come wuth me, Mr Galliah. And you, Miss Thruckmorton. I will need your help.

Sydney De Lainey, Maud and Mr Galley exit through the door UR. *With bad grace, Myrtle Throckmorton follows*

Monty Gus, Harry — go on. I've made myself look a juggins. Now it's your turn.

Harry Oh, all right. Come on, Gus.

Monty, Harry and Gus follow Myrtle Throckmorton out

Lydia Farrelly I hope there's something suitably alluring for Helena to wear.

Branston Parrish And I'd better see what Bottom's got apart from the Ass's Head.

Lydia Farrelly and Branston Parrish go out through the door UR

Lawrence enters through the door DL*. He looks as if he has just had a terrible shock*

Mrs Littlehouse (*not seeing him*) Well, I suppose the next thing we must do is ——

Lawrence (*authoritative, his shyness gone*) No. Now we must do nothing.

Mrs Littlehouse What?

Lawrence The king has been taken ill!

There is consternation amongst all on stage

There will be no coronation on Thursday.

Alexandra What's happened? What's wrong with him?

Lawrence I heard the news from a policeman. King Edward has had an operation for appendicitis.

Alexandra But is he well after the operation?

Lawrence His life is in the balance.

There are expressions of shock and concern from all

Maud What should we do?

Mrs Littlehouse We must stop our rehearsal.

Miss Horton Of course, it is not suitable in the circumstances.

Miss Sandwich No, of course not. (*Wringing her hands*) Oh dear. Is there nothing we can do?

Miss Brabazon Of course there is. We can pray. (*Moving to sit down at the piano*) We can pray for the life of His Majesty. (*She begins to play "God Save The King"*)

Gradually, everyone on stage stands to attention and joins in, with complete seriousness. They start quietly, but by the end, the noise is very loud

All   God save our gracious King!
                       Long live our noble King!
                       God save the King!
                       Send him victorious,
                       Happy and glorious,
                       Long to reign over us:
                       God save the King!

                       O Lord our God arise,
                       Scatter his enemies
                       And make them fall;
                       Confound their politics,
                       Frustrate their knavish tricks,
                       On Thee our hopes we fix:
                       God save the King!

*The mood has changed completely. After Miss Brabazon has hit the final
notes, everyone on stage — apart from Lawrence, who does not move —
serious, subdued, dabbing at eyes with handkerchiefs, heads out through
the doors* UR *and* UL, *Alexandra at the rear*

Lawrence Alexandra …

*Alexandra stops and looks back at him. For a moment there is eye contact.
Then, slowly and sadly she shakes her head, and goes on out through the
door* UR

Lawrence lowers his head in misery

Maud comes bursting in through the door UL

Maud Where is he? Where is he?
Lawrence Who, Mrs De Lainey? Who are you looking for?
Maud My husband! I know it! He's with that good-for-nothing minx, Miss
Farrelly!
Lawrence Mrs De Lainey, this is no time for such thoughts. There is terrible
news that ——
Maud (*not listening to him*) I'll find him! He and the hussy will be in here!
(*She pulls open the curtain to the ladies' — i.e. left-hand — compartment*)

*Sure enough, Lydia Farrelly is discovered in a clinch. But the other
participant is Monty, in his Puck outfit. Both leap apart in embarrassment
as the curtain is opened*

Monty Oh, crikey!

Maud Not there! I'll find him, though. He must be in this one! (*She pulls open the curtain to the gentlemen's compartment*)

And sure enough, her husband is there. Sydney De Lainey is slumped in a chair, dead. One of the prop swords is stuck in his chest; there is a lot of blood on his shirt-front. At his feet is the box which contained the two diamond crowns. It is open and empty

It takes a moment for this image to register on Maud De Lainey. Then she screams

The CURTAIN *falls*

ACT II
SCENE 1

The same. It is Monday, 15th September 1902

The changing compartments are still up in the Committee Room, but with all their curtains drawn back. King Edward VII's picture is still on the back wall, but the coronation bunting has been taken down. A copy of the day's "The Times" newspaper has been left on a chair

When the CURTAIN *rises, Branston Parrish is holding court to Mrs Littlehouse, Miss Horton, Miss Sandwich and Myrtle Throckmorton*

Branston Parrish And there's another song here, which I think could fit in frightfully well. Listen out, ladies. (*To Mrs Littlehouse*) I think you will enjoy this one, light of my life.

Mrs Littlehouse blushes

> (*Singing: a verse and chorus from G.W. Hunter's song "Funny Things They Do Upon the Sly"*)
>> There's the parson who's supposed to be so good,
>> Do wrong you'd really think he never could,
>> But now and then we read
>> Of some very funny deed,
>> That a parson's done, but which he never should;
>
> (*With a meaningful glance at Miss Horton*)
>> There's the stiff old maid, who likes to fume and boil,
>> She's been made so long, she's very apt to spoil,
>> Secretly she'll plan
>> To try and trap a man,
>> She's equal to a dose of castor oil:
>> If she could grab a man and lock him up,
>> When not another living soul was nigh,
>> She's take away his breath,
>> She'd squeeze the man to death,
>> Such funny things are done upon the sly.
>
> (*He finishes in a pose with his arms out*)

Mrs Littlehouse claps vigorously. Myrtle Throckmorton starts clapping.
Miss Horton gives Myrtle Throckmorton a deterring glance and she stops.
Miss Horton and Miss Sandwich very pointedly do not clap

Miss Horton I think that's an extremely vulgar song.

Branston Parrish Only, I dare say, because it comes a bit close to home, Miss Horton. Lines about spinsters trying to trap men.

Miss Horton Nonsense, Mr Parrish. I have never in my life tried to trap a man.

Branston Parrish Never succeeded, anyway. *(To Mrs Littlehouse)* Spanking good song, though, ain't it?

Mrs Littlehouse Well ——

Miss Sandwich I think you're fortunate that Miss Brabazon is not here. She would be deeply offended by lines about parsons misbehaving.

Branston Parrish Same story. She'd only be offended because no parson's ever misbehaved with her.

Miss Horton Please let's have no more of this. We are all agreed, Mr Parrish, that what you have just sung is a vulgar song.

Branston Parrish And Bottom is a vulgar character. That's the point.

Miss Horton But a song like that does not belong amidst the poetry of William Shakespeare's *A Midsummer Night's Dream*.

Branston Parrish I think it does. What's your view, Constantia, my essence of summer-dew?

Mrs Littlehouse *(simpering)* Oh ... *(In something of a cleft stick)* Well, Branston, it's a ... It's a very amusing song — but I think Miss Horton may have a point. Does it really fit into *A Midsummer Night's Dream*?

Branston Parrish Of course it does. All the characters are doing funny things upon the sly — that's what the play's about.

Mrs Littlehouse I agree, but ...

Branston Parrish So it'd make very good sense for Bottom to sing this song. And I'm sure I can persuade Miss Brabazon to play it for me — if I turn the full focus of my charm upon her.

Miss Horton I very much doubt the efficacy of such a procedure, Mr Parrish.

Branston Parrish Well, what it I offered to pay her extra?

Miss Horton Yes, that would probably do the trick.

Branston Parrish Pity we haven't got the orchestra Mr De Lainey was going to pay for. I'd like to do that song with a full orchestra.

Mrs Littlehouse But, Branston, I must ask you — where would the song fit into the play?

Branston Parrish *(picking up his copy of the play)* Oh, I've worked that out. When Bottom wakes Titania. You see, it's what Shakespeare intended — he's given Bottom a song to sing there. And it begins, "The ousel cock so black of hue ..." Now that may have had great significance in Shakespeare's time — riotously funny it probably was, had the groundlings rolling in the aisles, they were no doubt telling ousel cock jokes all the time — but it doesn't mean a dicky-bird to an audience in the reign of King Edward VII, does it ... ?

Mrs Littlehouse Perhaps not.

Branston Parrish O my glimmer of an Orient pearl ——

Mrs Littlehouse (*simpering*) Oh ...

Branston Parrish (*pressing home his advantage*) Whereas G.W. Hunter's "Funny Things They Do Upon The Sly" will really hit the spot.

Miss Horton Mr Parrish, this is the Bellingford Amateur Dramaticks, not the Bellingford Amateur Music Hall Society.

Branston Parrish I know the song'll work. Come on, Constantia, you tiger-lily of man's desiring, come through to the hall and hear it on stage. Then you'll get the full picture.

Mrs Littlehouse (*weakening in the face of his flattery*) Well, yes, we really should be starting rehearsal. I've called the other actors for different times ...

Branston Parrish Listen to my song first, my essence of rose-petals.

Mrs Littlehouse (*simpering*) I'm not entirely convinced it's going to be the right thing ...

Branston Parrish (*leading the way to the door* UR) I'll convince you. There are another four verses you ain't heard yet. Come along, Myrtle. You help convince her.

Myrtle Throckmorton I'm not sure ...

Branston Parrish Please. Let me sing my song to two of the world's most beautiful women.

Myrtle Throckmorton (*rendered quite skittish by the compliment*) Oh. Very well, if you insist ...

Branston Parrish stands at the door and bows. Mrs Littlehouse and Myrtle Throckmorton go through into the Hall. With a smug grin back at Miss Horton, Branston Parrish follows them

Miss Horton Well, Miss Sandwich. We seem to have escaped the frying-pan, only to have landed firmly in the fire.

Miss Sandwich Oh yes, indeed, Miss Horton.

Miss Horton Mr De Lainey cut down *A Midsummer Night's Dream* so that only he had any significant lines — while now Mr Parrish seems determined to inflate the play out of all proportion with low comic songs.

Miss Sandwich Yes.

Miss Horton And Mrs Littlehouse is so besotted by his ridiculous compliments that she will not oppose his slightest whim. I don't know what's to be done.

Miss Sandwich Oh, dear. Still, at least you have got your part of Hippolyta back.

Miss Horton Yes, but how long will it be before the Queen of the Amazons is forced into singing the songs of Miss Marie Lloyd or Miss Vesta Tilley?

Miss Sandwich (*hopefully*) Of course, Vesta Tilley dresses up as a man, doesn't she?

Miss Horton Of what relevance is that, Miss Sandwich?

Miss Sandwich I was thinking it might render my playing of Flute the Bellows-mender a little more respectable.

Miss Horton Nothing, Miss Sandwich, that emanates from the Music Hall can ever be deemed respectable.

Miss Sandwich (*her hopes dashed*) No, of course not, Miss Horton (*Seeing* The Times *on the chair and picking it up*) Oh, Mr Parrish has left his *Times*. (*She opens it and starts to flick through the pages*)

Miss Horton What are you looking for?

Miss Sandwich I always like to look at the Reports of Criminal Trials.

Miss Horton Do you, Miss Sandwich? Is this in the expectation of recognizing the names of your close relatives?

Miss Sandwich Certainly not, Miss Horton. It is in expectation of seeing a report of poor Mr Galley's trial.

Miss Horton You should not refer to a convicted murderer as *poor* Mr Galley.

Miss Sandwich But he's not convicted.

Miss Horton Yet. The trial will be a formality.

Miss Sandwich Suppose he didn't do it?

Miss Horton I hope, Miss Sandwich, you are not suggesting that a member of the Bellingford Amateur Dramaticks might have killed Mr De Lainey. Mr Galley is a member of the servant-class. Obviously he's the murderer. Soon he will be hanged for his crime. And serve him right.

Miss Sandwich (*with less certainty*) Yes ... (*Finding her place in the paper*) Ah. (*She reads*) No, there's only some man accused of stealing billiard balls. (*She puts the paper back down on the chair, still folded open at the page she was reading*)

Miss Horton It's disgusting. Billiard balls. What will they think of stealing next? I'm certain there's been more crime since King Edward's been on the throne.

Miss Sandwich Oh, I don't think you can say that, Miss Horton.

Miss Horton I just have said it, Miss Sandwich. And I'm sure I'm right. There are a lot of unpleasantnesses around today that wouldn't have been tolerated in Queen Victoria's time. The forces of anarchy are gathering. And I'm not sure that all's well with the Empire.

Lawrence enters from the door DL. *As ever, he is carrying a book, and he looks rather glum*

Lawrence Ah, good-evening, ladies.

Miss Horton Mr Furze.

Miss Sandwich Good-evening, Mr Furze. We were just discussing Mr Galley.

Miss Horton (*slightly miffed at her friend taking the conversational initiative from her*) Yes, we were.

Miss Sandwich I was wondering ... Are you convinced of his guilt, Mr Furze?

Lawrence S-S-S-certainly not. There's no real evidence against him.

Miss Horton There is logic against him.

Lawrence looks uncertain

Oh, for goodness' sake. We were all here when Mr De Lainey met Mr Galley, apparently for the first time. There was no question but that they recognized each other. Then we hear from the police that Mr Galley had a previous conviction for the theft of jewellery; that he was transported to Australia for the crime; that when his seven years' sentence was up he returned to this country and changed his name to procure employment in the Institute under false pretences ... I think it's very difficult to have any other suspects, Mr Furze.

Lawrence It's still all s-s-s-s-s-circumstantial.

Miss Horton Mr Galley murdered Mr De Lainey. There is nothing else to think.

Lawrence But if there was one shred of actual evidence that ——

From off L comes the sound of the De Laineys' motor car approaching

Miss Horton Oh dear. Here comes that wretched Mrs De Lainey and her daughters. I don't feel like facing them.

Miss Sandwich But we must face them, Miss Horton. It is only three months since her husband's death. We must still show her respect and consideration.

Miss Horton Huh. I might feel that, if she showed a little respect and consideration for her husband's memory. To be continuing the performance of amateur dramatics while still in mourning, to my mind betrays a total lack of refinement.

Miss Sandwich She said she and the girls had to continue, because it was what Mr De Lainey would have liked.

Miss Horton I'm glad we don't have to follow that through in everything. (*Darkly*) From what I hear, there are certain things Mr De Lainey liked which have absolutely no place in polite society. (*Moving suddenly towards the door* DR) Look out, they're coming. Excuse us, Mr Furze.

Miss Horton and Miss Sandwich scuttle off through the door DR

Lawrence contemplates running off himself, but decides not to and stands, awkwardly

Maud De Lainey enters, leads in Alexandra, Arabella, Amelia, Alberta and Daisy. They are all dressed in mourning black — ideally their dresses should be exactly the same design as each of them wore in Act I — and Amelia, Alberta and Daisy each carry animal baskets

Lawrence Mrs De Lainey.

Maud (*inclining her head to Lawrence without enthusiasm*) Mr Furze.

Daisy Mr Furze, I've bwought more of my wabbits with me. My wabbits are going to have a wehearsal too. Won't that be wipping?

Lawrence I'm sure it will, Daisy.

Maud (*to the girls; sternly*) We will all go straight through to the hall, if you please. I want to practise ballet steps with the little ones. (*She stalks up towards the exit* UL)

Alexandra makes to follow

Lawrence Alexandra ...

Maud stands implacably by the door. Alexandra avoids Lawrence's eye, and goes out through the door. With one more deterring look to Lawrence, Maud goes after her, followed by Amelia, Alberta and Daisy

Arabella lingers, and comes towards Lawrence

Lawrence Miss Arabella, what was Alexandra's response?

Arabella (*handing an unopened letter across to him*) She wouldn't even read it.

Lawrence Ah. Very well. Thank you for trying.

Arabella I'm sorry.

Lawrence S-So am I, but ... And is young Mr Harry Trunchpole still in favour?

Arabella He visits the house quite frequently.

Lawrence (*with a hurt nod*) Mm. Thank you, Miss Arabella.

Arabella turns as if to join her family, then makes a decision and turns back

Arabella Mr Furze, do you believe that Mr Galley killed my father?

Lawrence I can understand why the police believe it.

Arabella That is an answer to a different question.

Lawrence Yes, you are right. Very well, Miss Arabella. I don't believe that Mr Galley killed your father.

Arabella Then who did? Please, Mr Furze. Be my Sherlock Holmes, solve my father's murder.

Lawrence (*unable to resist her appeal*) All right. Let us begin by thinking who had the opportunity to commit the murder ... (*He walks round the stage as he thinks during the following*) Well, assuming your father met his end where he was found, in this dressing compartment here ... He must have come in through the central doors — because he would have been seen if he'd come through either of the others ...

Arabella So his murderer must have come in by the same way ...?

Lawrence Yes. And ... Do you realize a terrible thing, Miss Arabella?

Arabella What?

Lawrence Your father must have met his end while those of us in here were singing *God Save the King*. Our singing must have drowned the noise of his killing.

Arabella That's frightful.

Lawrence So the villain added sacrilege to the crime of murder. Well, we know who was here singing for the king's good health ...

Arabella Which, heavens be praised, has been restored. He's now safely crowned and as well as ever.

Lawrence Yes. So who wasn't in this committee room at the relevant time ...? Mr Galley, obviously ...

Arabella Harry, Monty and Gus ...

Lawrence Right. Branston Parrish ... Miss Farrelly ...

Arabella Mama ...

Lawrence I'm sorry. I'm afraid she must go on our list of suspects too. Who else? I'm sure there's someone we've forgotten.

Arabella No, I don't think so ... (*Trying to think*) Well, there's ... Myrtle! Myrtle Throckmorton.

Lawrence Oh yes, Myrtle. It's somehow easy to forget Myrtle, isn't it? Well, I'd say that's plenty of suspects. If we exclude Mr Galley — which we must do for this exercise ...

Arabella We've still got seven potential murderers.

Lawrence Very well, let's move on to motives. Who would have a reason to want your father dead?

Arabella Mr Galley. Because Papa could have made public his crimes and the fact that he was living under an assumed name.

Lawrence We're putting Mr Galley on one side, though. Harry Trunchpole had already got his eye on Alexandra, and was getting a pretty dusty response from your father to his interest ...

Arabella Yes, so he had a motive. He's doing much better with his courtship since Papa's death. Obviously no engagement could be announced while we're still in mourning, but — Mama has implied that, as soon as it is appropriate ...

Lawrence (*pained by this and moving on quickly*) Then Augustus Tarleton appeared to be in some sort of financial mess ...

Arabella So he could have committed the murder to steal the crowns and sell them.

Lawrence Mm. Because, of course, the crowns never have been found, have they? What about Monty?

Arabella The fact that he was discovered kissing Miss Farrelly might seem to eliminate both of them as suspects.

Lawrence Neither having had time to do the deed?

Arabella nods

Possibly. And I can't really envisage Monty managing his first kiss and his first murder at the same time. (*Approaching the subject rather carefully*) Of course, when we come on to Miss Farrelly ...

Arabella You don't need to beat about the bush, Mr Furze. I am not completely innocent, and am aware that Papa's behaviour was not always above reproach.

Lawrence Good. I am relieved to hear that.

Arabella He had definitely met Miss Farrelly before — somewhere. Which would also be a reason why Mama might have had a motive to kill him — for the hurt he had done to her reputation.

Lawrence (*looking at Arabella with admiration*) For your age, you're a very mature young woman, Miss Arabella.

Arabella Thank you. Come on, more motives.

Lawrence Branston Parrish had wanted to play Bottom all of his life, and your father had cut the part down to mere scraps.

Arabella And Myrtle Throckmorton had lost her part completely. I gather she had always been prompter for other productions of the Bellingford Amateur Dramaticks. Then the first time she gets her own speaking part, Papa snatches it away from her.

Lawrence Mind you, nature had not formed her to be the ideal Mustardseed.

Arabella No. Daisy's much better. But Myrtle's a very romantic soul. She goes through life dreaming she's about to meet some handsome lover who will lay down his life for her. But she's also the kind of girl for whom the smallest slight can cut pretty deep. I can imagine Myrtle nurturing murderous thoughts.

Lawrence And of course, in the recent redistribution of parts in the play, Miss Horton got Hippolyta back, and Myrtle Throckmorton took over as Peter Quince. So Myrtle has directly benefited from your father's death. (*Thoughtfully*) Hm ... Seven people — eight if we include Mr Galley — who might have wanted to kill Sydney De Lainey.

Arabella It is not the most ringing endorsement of anyone's personality, is it? Mr Furze, I know Papa was not an entirely admirable man — could in fact be an extremely silly man — but that does not mean I did not love him ...

Lawrence Of course not, Miss Arabella. (*Seeing* The Times *where it was left on the chair*) Great Scott!

Arabella What is it?

Lawrence (*picking up the paper and reading; enormously excited*) This is it! This is what we've been waiting for! This means it works!

Arabella I'm afraid, Mr Furze, I have no idea what you're talking about.

Lawrence Listen. (*Reading*) "Harry Jackson, forty-one, labourer, was indicted for a burglary at Denmark Hill …"

Arabella (*still confused*) Indeed?

Lawrence (*continuing to read*) "Mr Muir, who prosecuted for the Treasury, said the case was an ordinary one but for the fact that *the fingerprints would be given in evidence for the purpose of connecting the prisoner with the burglary.*" Do you see? Do you see!

Arabella No.

Alexandra enters through the door UL

During the following, Alexandra tries to attract Arabella's attention, but her sister is too caught up in Lawrence's exhilaration to notice

Lawrence (*reading with intense excitement*) "On the morning of June 27th it was discovered that the house at Denmark Hill had been entered by burglars, and some billiard balls stolen. One of the burglars had left imprints of his fingers, and a particularly plain imprint of his left thumb, on the newly painted window sills. Sergeant Collins" — that's Charles Stockley Collins, I know him! — "an expert in fingerprints, took photographs of the prints, and, on examining them with some prints in the possession of the police of the prisoner's fingers, he came to the conclusion *that both were from the same hand'*!"

Alexandra, caught up in the excitement, moves closer

Alexandra You mean it works? It actually works?

Lawrence is so caught up in his excitement that he puts his arms around the two girls and dances a little jig of glee with them

Lawrence Yes, it works! It works! (*Managing to read while still dancing around with the girls*) "The jury found the prisoner 'Guilty', and several previous convictions were proved against him. The Common Sergeant sentenced the prisoner to seven years' penal servitude"! Charles'll be as pleased as Punch! The first successful conviction on fingerprint evidence in a British court! Oh, this is a bit of all right, and no mistake! (*He realizes* *what he's doing and slows down. He looks at the two girls in his arms and releases them)*

Alexandra, who had been enjoying what was happening, straightens her clothes primly

I'm very s-s-s-s-s-sorry.

Alexandra (*formally*) Thank you, Mr Furze. Your apology is accepted. Arabella, Mama requires your presence to practise the "Philomel with melody" dance.

Arabella (*rushing very quickly* UL, *hoping to leave them together*)
   "I go, I go — look how I go ——
   Swifter than an arrow from Tartar's bow."

Arabella exits UL

There is an awkward silence

Alexandra Mrs Littlehouse says the rehearsal is running a little late. When Harry, Monty and Gus come, could you tell them they won't be needed for another half-hour?

Lawrence Yes. I will. Alexandra …

Alexandra I must go — back to the dance rehearsal.

Lawrence But you're not in any of the dances.

Alexandra No … But — Mama needs my support.

Lawrence Alexandra …

Alexandra (*formally*) I'm delighted that your friend has had such a success with his fingerprinting system of criminal investigation.

Lawrence Yes. I must get an evening paper to see if there's any more about the s-s-s-s-s—— (*He stutters under the following*)

Alexandra Excuse me.

Alexandra exits through the door UL

Lawrence (*miserably*) — story. (*He moves towards the door* DL *with a melancholy shake of his head*)

Harry, Monty and Gus enter DL, *meeting Lawrence*

Good-evening, gentlemen.

Harry, Monty and Gus nod at Lawrence rather patronizingly

If anyone's looking for me, I've just gone out for a paper.

Gus We'll tell 'em — in the unlikely event that anyone *is* looking for you.

Lawrence (*deliberately not rising to this rudeness*) And, by-the-by, Mrs Littlehouse says she won't be needing you for rehearsal for another half-hour.

Monty Dash it. I put on a real head of steam to get here in time.

Lawrence makes to leave, then has another thought

Lawrence Might I just ask you s-s-something ...?

Gus Don't see why you should.

Harry No, of course you may. Ask, and it shall be given you.

Lawrence Thank you. I was just having a conversation about the night Mr De Lainey died.

Gus Were you, by George?

Lawrence And we were discussing whereabouts in the Institute everyone was at that moment.

Monty (*embarrassedly*) Well, I was — as a matter of fact — sort of ——

Lawrence I know where you were, Mr Pottle.

Monty (*with relief*) Righty-ho.

Lawrence But I don't know where you two gentlemen were.

Gus My God, are you turning detective? That fellow Conan Doyle has a lot to answer for — giving accounts clerks the illusion that they can be Sherlock Holmes. I'm damned if I'm going to answer your questions.

Harry I'll answer for you then, Gus. I'll tell Mr Furze what we told the police when they asked the same question. Mr Augustus Tarleton and I had gone through into the hall to find out the worst about the costumes we were expected to wear in *A Midsummer Night's Dream*.

Lawrence S-so you were with all the others who had gone through there?

Harry No. We'd wanted to — exchange views on the costumes without offending the ears of the ladies. So we went to talk in the foyer — you know, up the other end of the hall.

Lawrence And you were there, together, all the time?

Harry (*looking steadily at Lawrence*) Yes.

Gus (*sending Lawrence up*) S-s-so you must look s-s-s-somewhere else for your murderous s-s-s-scoundrel, mustn't you, Mr Furze?

Lawrence Yes, Mr Tarleton. (*He heads for the exit* DL) And s-s-s-so I shall.

Lawrence exits through the door DL

The three young men left on stage chuckle

Monty Blighter's got a cheek, hasn't he?

Gus Thinking he has the right to ask us questions like that ... Oiks like that ought to know their place.

Harry Careful what you say, Gus.

Gus Why?

Harry I told you before. We're entering the century of the working man.

Gus Heaven forbid. Give the working man any power at all, and the anarchists'll take over. My view is that all working men should be strangled at birth.

Harry One of the qualities I've always admired in you, Gus, is your tolerance.

Gus and Harry both chuckle

Monty It really gives me the pip that we've got to wait around for half an hour. Don't they realize that gentlemen have other demands on their time?

Gus What other demands do you have on your time, Monty?

Monty Well, I ... (*He can't think of any*) That's not the dashed point. What're we going to do for half an hour?

Gus Could go to that public house down the road and sink a few brandies.

Harry I didn't really get the impression we were particularly welcome there last time. Full of costers, tinkers and bargees. We were just a fraction too clean and well-spoken for their taste, I thought.

Gus Suppose you're right. Kind of dive you could easily come out of and find your dashed wallet's missing.

Harry At least you seem to have something in your wallet these days, Gus.

Gus (*with a chuckle*) Yes, dashed convenient when an aged relative dies, ain't it?

Monty I say, I've had a thought!

Harry If it maintains your usual standard, Monty, I suggest you keep it to yourself.

Monty No, this one's definitely up to sample. (*As if it's a stunningly original idea*) Why don't we have a game of Whiff-Waff?

Harry Ping-Pong, Monty. But no. Ping-Pong's such a bore. There's nothing so *passé* as yesterday's craze.

Monty Oh. So what's your craze now, Harry?

Harry Bridge.

Monty Hanged if I'm going to play Bridge. I'm no good at card games.

Gus You were no good at Ping-Pong, Monty.

Monty Ah, but I've been practising. With my mater. I could give anyone a run for their money now.

Gus Even the lovely Lydia.

Monty (*embarrassedly*) Well, yes. We have had a go on the table, actually.

Harry (*aware of the innuendo*) Have you, by George?

Monty (*furiously*) Now, listen, Harry, I must ask you to take that back!

Harry Oh?

Monty Dash it, you're talking about the woman I love! I won't have aspersions cast on the character of the sweetest, most innocent girl that was ever born!

Harry (*avoiding Gus's eye and trying not to laugh*) Lydia? No, no, of course not. Withdraw my remark absolutely.

Gus So how's it going, Monty — the course of that particular true love?

Monty Oh, Gus, it's topping. Lydia's an absolute corker.

Gus Couldn't agree more. You'd go along with that, wouldn't you, Harry?

Harry Indeed. As Tennyson put it, a man could "waste his whole heart in one kiss upon her perfect lips."

Monty (*embarrassed*) Mm. Well, I wouldn't know about that.

Harry Oh. Come on, Monty, you've kissed her.

Monty Yes, but just the once.

Harry Really?

Monty Well, the circumstances were dashed awkward. I mean, being discovered back there by Mrs De Lainey — and that just before her old man was found skewered. Bit of a damper to my — you know — and an even nastier shock for a sweet, sensitive, innocent girl like Lydia ——

Harry I'm sure it must have been.

Monty Not ideal circumstances for her first kiss, were they?

Harry Her first kiss?

This time he cannot avoid Gus's eye. They both have serious difficulty avoiding laughing out loud during the following

No, no, I can see that.

Monty So she's been a bit, sort of, well, upset by it all — and we haven't actually kissed again since.

Harry Ah.

Monty (*enthusiastically; daringly*) Still, when we're married, Lydia says I'll be able to kiss her any time I want.

Gus Does she?

Monty Yes. (*He gives a daring giggle*) Crikey, what a thought, eh?

Harry When you're married? Are you really intending to go through with this, Monty?

Monty Course I am, you chump. I can't imagine a better or cleverer or more beautiful or more innocent girl in the whole wide world to become my wife? Can you?

Harry (*still trying to avoid giggling*) No. Well, congratulations, old chap.

Monty Thank you.

Gus (*also having difficulty keeping a straight face*) Yes, good business.

Monty Thanks.

Harry (*after a slight pause*) Have you actually introduced Miss Farrelly to your mother yet?

Monty No. (*Proudly*) But Lydia's coming down to the Towers to meet Mater this weekend.

Harry Now that is an event for which I would pay to obtain tickets.

Gus Come on, chaps, I want a drink. Let's risk the costers, tinkers and bargees.

Monty Yes, I'm game for a peg.

Gus Harry?

Harry (*moving across to sit at the piano*) I'll sit this one out.

Gus Righty-ho. (*Moving across to the door* DL) I'll buy you a drink, Monty — (*for Harry's benefit*) to drink the health of you and your beautiful, unspoilt, innocent bride.

Gus and Monty exit

Harry chuckles. Then, he picks out the tune of "Bill Bailey, Won't You Please Come Home?" on the piano

A short time passes while he plays

Lydia Farrelly comes out of the door DR *and crosses to the piano*

Lydia Farrelly (*picking up the end of the tune and singing*)
           Bill Bailey, won't you please come home?
           Come home, Bill Bailey!
           Bill Bailey, won't you please come on home?
           Come on home!

Harry plays the final chords and looks up at her

Harry Lydia ... I gather congratulations are in order.

Lydia Farrelly Mm?

Harry You and Monty.

Lydia Farrelly Oh yes. Haven't quite got all the details sorted, but — (*with determination*) it'll happen.

Harry A marriage made in heaven. Monty's spent his entire life looking for "the best, cleverest, most beautiful and innocent girl in the whole wide world."

Lydia Farrelly Well, ain't it wonderful that he's found her?

Harry Oh, yes, yes. As I say, congratulations.

Lydia Farrelly Thank you, kind sir. And how about you and Alexandra?

Harry Going pretty well, I'd say.

Lydia Farrelly And have you had your — evening at Romano's — with her yet?

Harry No, deuce take it. Think that may have to wait till after the wedding.

Lydia Farrelly Ah.

Harry And I gather this weekend Monty's taking you to meet Lady Pottle
— or, as she's better known in our circles, "The Black Widow Spider".

Lydia Farrelly I have heard the nickname.

Harry So how're you going to manage that, Lydia?

Lydia Farrelly With perfect decorum, Harry. It's just another part, and in my
time I have played a great variety of parts. (*Making her accent a little more
upper-crust*) This one is: the perfect potential daughter-in-law.

Harry Are you going to introduce Lady Pottle to your parents — (*dropping
into Cockney*) down the Mile End Road?

Lydia Farrelly (*still in an upper-crust accent*) Sadly I cannot introduce my
parents. My mother was killed in a hunting accident, and my father gave
his life fighting for Queen and Country against General Botha's Boers at
Spioenkop.

Harry Good. Very good. Do you know, Lydia, I think you've got the nerve
to get away with it.

Lydia Farrelly Of course I have, Harry.

Harry Hm. So this means you won't need me to set you up in a flat in
Mayfair?

Lydia Farrelly If all goes according to plan, no.

Lawrence enters DL *with his evening paper. He stops and listens to the
conversation at the piano*

Harry But we still might meet, do you think — once you're safely married
to the Honourable Montague Pottle — and I'm safely married to Alexandra
De Lainey ...?

Lydia Farrelly (*after a moment, with a little mock-curtsy*) I'll instruct my
maid that I'm always in for Mr Harry Trunchpole.

*They chuckle in complicity. Lawrence looks furious, and makes to rush
across and say something*

Myrtle Throckmorton appears through the entrance UR

Lawrence stops

Myrtle Throckmorton Oh, Miss Farrelly, there you are. Mrs Littlehouse
wants to have a look at the argument between Helena and Hermia.

Lydia Farrelly (*making for the door*) I'll come.

Harry (*noticing Lawrence's presence*) Does she want a Demetrius too?

Myrtle Throckmorton She didn't say she did.

Harry (*deciding he'd rather not be left alone with Lawrence*) I'll come as well, in case I'm needed.

Lydia Farrelly and Harry exit into the hall

Lawrence reads his newspaper. Myrtle Throckmorton hovers, nervous and awkward

Myrtle Throckmorton (*after a moment*) Mr Furze …
Lawrence (*looking up from his paper*) Yes?
Myrtle Throckmorton Miss De Lainey was talking through there — about this fingerprint business ——
Lawrence It's a wonderful innovation. Will turn the world of criminal investigation on its head.
Myrtle Throckmorton — and she said that people who've done something wrong — leave traces — and will inevitably be caught — and can never get away with anything …
Lawrence That's the idea of the system, yes.
Myrtle Throckmorton (*crying*) Oh, Mr Furze, I feel so guilty. I've done wrong.
Lawrence (*moving to comfort her*) What have you done wrong, Miss Throckmorton?
Myrtle Throckmorton That night — when we heard that the coronation had been postponed — the night Mr De Lainey — died …
Lawrence Yes?
Myrtle Throckmorton I did something wrong — and I haven't told anyone — because I thought no-one would ever find out — but now — (*crying more*) there's my fingerprints all over everything — and I'll be caught out in my lies …
Lawrence What did you do, Miss Throckmorton? What did you lie about?
Myrtle Throckmorton Well … When the police asked me — I told them I hadn't seen anyone through in the hall, but — in fact, there's a cubby-hole just by the side of the stage — where all the gubbins for the Institute is kept …
Lawrence I've seen it, yes.
Myrtle Throckmorton Well, he'd kept asking me if I'd go in there with him — and I kept saying no — and then that evening, I'd got the hump because Mr De Lainey had said I couldn't play Mustardseed — and I was feeling bad — and I thought — what if I'm never in my life going to get a man either — so I agreed to go into the cubby-hole with him — and so I lied when I said I didn't see anyone. I was kissing and cuddling all the time while Mr De Lainey was being killed — and my fingerprints are all over the cubby-hole and soon everybody will know what I've done!

Lawrence They won't necessarily, Miss Throckmorton. We can probably keep it quiet.

Myrtle Throckmorton (*pathetically grateful*) Oh, do you think you can?

Lawrence I'll do my best. Tell me, though — who were you in the cubby-hole with?

Myrtle Throckmorton Well, obviously ... Mr Galley.

Lawrence (*who hadn't expected this*) Really? But why didn't he say? If you were with him all the time, then he couldn't have been the one who murdered Mr De Lainey.

Myrtle Throckmorton I know. (*Now blissfully and romantically full of herself*) Mr Galley behaved rather magnificently. He had to decide which he valued more — his life or my reputation. And I'm glad to say ... what he really valued ... was my reputation.

Lawrence But, Miss Throckmorton, we can't allow a man to go for the gallows for ——

Branston Parrish, sounding very excited, is heard approaching the door UL

Quick, come with me. We must talk further.

Lawrence hustles Myrtle Throckmorton off through the door DR

Branston Parrish enters through the door UL, *followed by an adoring Mrs Littlehouse and a very disapproving Miss Horton, together with an equally disapproving Miss Sandwich*

Branston Parrish (*going to the piano and riffling through some sheet music on top of it*) Now this is the one. You listen to this, my elixir of angels' wings.

Mrs Littlehouse (*feebly*) I'm not sure that we've really got the time for any more songs in the play, Branston.

Miss Horton No, we most certainly haven't.

Branston Parrish Just listen to it first. This one fits in perfectly.

Miss Sandwich Where does it fit in perfectly?

Branston Parrish Right at the end. After Bottom and his chums have done their *Pyramus and Thisbe*. It'll give a real rousing finish to their play.

Miss Horton This is ridiculous!

Branston Parrish (*ignoring Miss Horton*) Now listen to this, my little breath of gossamer moonlight.

Mrs Littlehouse (*simpering*) Oooh ...

Branston Parrish It's Fred Coyne's song: "The Tuner's Oppor-Tuner-Ty!"
(*Singing*) Miss Crochety Quaver was sweet seventeen,
        And a player of excellent skill.
        She would play all the day, all the ev'ning as well,

Making all the neighbourhood ill.
And to keep her piano in tune she would have
A good tuner constantly there,
(*With heavy innuendo*)
And he'd pull up the instrument three times a week,
Just to keep it in proper repair.
And first he'd tune it gently, then he'd tune it strong,
Then he'd touch a short note, then he'd run along,
Then he'd go with vengeance enough to break a key,
At last he tuned whene'er he got an oppor – tuner – ty!
(*He ends the song in a pose with his arms outstretched. Speaking*) There!
How'd you like that? Real bobby-dazzler, ain't it?

*Mrs Littlehouse looks on bemused, while Miss Horton and Miss Sandwich
look on appalled*

The CURTAIN *falls*

SCENE 2

The same. Tuesday, 12th November 1902. Evening

*The first performance of the Bellingford Amateur Dramaticks' "A Midsummer
Night's Dream" is under way. The Committee Room has not changed much
since the previous scene, though all the curtains of the changing compartments
are now closed, and the central doors into the hall are slightly open. There
is a jug of lemonade and glasses on a tray on top of the piano*

The CURTAIN *rises. Then Lawrence, dressed in his Lysander costume and
wearing heavy stage make-up, comes out of the male changing compartment,
closing the curtain behind him. He carries an envelope full of papers. He goes
across to the female changing compartment and coughs discreetly*

Lawrence (*in a whisper*) Miss Throckmorton.

*Myrtle Throckmorton appears out of the female compartment, closing the
curtain behind her. She also wears heavy make-up, and is dressed as Peter
Quince, in an Athenian tunic, leggings and a large bumpkin's straw hat.
The costume cannot be said to do much for her*

Myrtle Throckmorton Mr Furze.
Lawrence (*gesturing her down to the edge of the stage and speaking
confidentially*) I'm sorry I was unable to speak to you earlier. There were
too many people about.
Myrtle Throckmorton Yes.

Lawrence But I am glad now to be able to tell you that I have all the information I require.

Myrtle Throckmorton To track down the murderer?

Lawrence Yes. A package of papers was sent here by my friend Detective-Sergeant Charles Stockley Collins. It only just arrived by messenger.

Myrtle Throckmorton And it proves who killed Mr De Lainey?

Lawrence Not completely. But it gives a very strong indication of who might have committed the crime. Certainly of who had the strongest motive.

Myrtle Throckmorton So how will you be able to prove it?

Lawrence I'm not sure. Obviously, if the murderer confessed in front of the whole company, that would be proof enough.

Myrtle Throckmorton But is he likely to do that?

Lawrence Or is *she* likely to do that?

Myrtle Throckmorton (*taking in the implication of what he's said*) Ah.

Lawrence I do have an idea of how I may extract a confession from our murderer, though I'm not sure it's going to work. But did you fulfil your part of our bargain, Miss Throckmorton?

Myrtle Throckmorton (*with a sigh*) Yes, I did. It was not easy, but I have done as you requested.

Lawrence And your word was believed?

Myrtle Throckmorton It was.

Lawrence Have you made the other arrangements I requested?

Myrtle Throckmorton I have.

Lawrence Good. You did well.

Myrtle Throckmorton (*relieved to have met his demands*) Thank you, Mr Furze.

Lawrence I will require one more thing from you, though, Miss Throckmorton.

Myrtle Throckmorton Of course. But please call me "Myrtle".

Lawrence I will happily call you "Myrtle". And you may call me "Lawrence".

Myrtle Throckmorton Thank you. So what was it you wanted from me, Lawrence?

Lawrence A powder-puff. And a box of powder.

Myrtle Throckmorton Why? I can see no flaws in your make-up.

Lawrence It's not for that. All will be explained shortly. Do you have a powder-puff and a box of powder that you can lend me?

Myrtle Throckmorton Yes, indeed. I will fetch them this instant. (*She goes into the female compartment*)

Lawrence crosses to the piano, picks up one of the glasses on the lemonade tray, lifts it up to look at the light through it, smiles with satisfaction and puts it down. Myrtle Throckmorton comes back out of the female compartment, with the powder and powder-puff, and closes the curtain behind her

Myrtle Throckmorton Here it is, Lawrence.

Lawrence Thank you very much, Myrtle. (*He puts the powder-box and puff on top of the piano*)

Myrtle Throckmorton And when do you plan your unmasking of the murderer to take place?

Lawrence It will have to be very soon, I'm afraid. When the members of the cast come off for the interval.

Myrtle Throckmorton Could it not wait till the end of the performance? This is the first night, after all.

Lawrence I'm afraid it could not. If the murderer gets wind of what I am preparing, all will be lost.

Myrtle Throckmorton Oh dear.

Lawrence Why are you upset, Myrtle?

Myrtle Throckmorton Because I've waited so long. This is my first chance with a speaking part in a Bellingford Amateur Dramaticks production, and it looks as if it may be cut short. Peter Quince has that wonderful introduction to the play of *Pyramus and Thisbe* in Act Five, which I would have hoped might achieve a great deal of laughter.

Lawrence Myrtle, there are some things in life that are more important than Amateur Dramatics.

Myrtle Throckmorton (*to whom this idea had never occurred*) Are there?

Miss Horton and Miss Sandwich enter through the door DL. *They are both heavily made up and in costume, Miss Horton as a rather imaginative version of the Queen of the Amazons (with a fake-looking crown), Miss Sandwich in her Flute outfit (beneath which she still insists on wearing her skirt)*

Miss Horton So — how is our first performance going?

Lawrence Very well, so far, I believe. The audience seemed to find we young lovers diverting. They even laughed in some of the right places.

Miss Sandwich They've laughed a lot in our scenes, the ones with the "rude mechanicals". And Mr Parrish received a round of applause.

Miss Horton (*venomously*) Did he? When?

Miss Sandwich When he sang "She Does The Fandango All Over the Place".

Miss Horton (*furiously*) This is too much! That man has ruined our play! It has become a mere Music Hall bill with Shakespeare acting as Master of Ceremonies! Oh, Mr Parrish drives me to distraction! Since Mr De Lainey died, Mr Parrish seems to have a mesmeric power over Mrs Littlehouse. You might almost imagine he planned Mr De Lainey's death with that outcome in mind!

There is an awkward silence. Then general throat-clearing

Miss Horton (*realizing what she's said*) That is to say — I didn't mean ...

Daisy enters UR *followed by Alberta, Amelia and Arabella. All are dressed like Arthur Rackham fairies*

Daisy (*in a panic*) Oh no! Wun of my wabbits has wun away! It's Wedvers. I'm afwaid he may have wun out into the woad! We must find Wedvers!

Daisy exits through the door DL, *followed by Alberta and Amelia*

Arabella joins the group on stage

Arabella I never thought it was a good idea to have live rabbits on stage.
Miss Sandwich Mr Beerbohm Tree always does.
Arabella But there is a difference between the technical resources of His Majesty's Theatre and the Bellingford Jubilee Institute.
Miss Sandwich If you are here, Miss Arabella, does it mean that we have reached the interval?
Arabella Not yet.
Miss Sandwich But as I recall, William Shakespeare's *A Midsummer Night's Dream* Act Three Scene One concludes: "Exit Titania with Bottom and the Fairies."
Arabella That may happen in William Shakespeare's *A Midsummer Night's Dream*. In Mr Branston Parrish's *A Midsummer Night's Dream* events occur rather differently.
Miss Horton I thought I knew about all the fatuous interpolations he has shoehorned into the play.
Arabella This one only went in this morning. Mrs Littlehouse was somehow persuaded to ——
Miss Horton (*putting her hands over her ears*) Don't tell me. I do not wish to hear.
Miss Sandwich (*fearing the worst*) How does the scene end now, Miss Arabella?
Arabella Bottom makes a braying noise. Titania says, "Tie up my lover's tongue; bring him silently."
Miss Sandwich Which are the last lines of Shakespeare's scene.
Arabella Yes. But in tonight's Bellingford Amateur Dramaticks' version, Bottom then says, "No, let's have a song first. You better nip orf, fairies — not suitable for your young ears." And then he sings a song.
Miss Sandwich Which song?
Miss Horton I do not wish to know. I've already heard as much as I can tolerate.

The sound of enthusiastic applause is heard from the Hall

Lawrence It sounds as though the audience liked it. (*To Miss Horton*) Why don't you get some lemonade before the rush?
Miss Horton I think I will. I need something, or I'll very soon be prostrate with aggravated neuritis. Come along, Miss Sandwich.
Arabella (*to Lawrence; in a whisper*) Have you had any luck?
Lawrence (*in a whisper*) The information has arrived. Everything is in readiness.
Arabella Well done. I'm sure it's going to work, Mr Furze.
Lawrence Let us hope so.

Branston Parrish bursts through the door, followed by Maud. He is dressed in an Athenian tunic and sandals, and is holding the ass's head under his arm. She is in Arthur Rackham-style fairy costume like her daughters; she wears a crown, but it is not as splendid as the missing one. At a distance follows Miss Brabazon, looking extremely sour. As the door opens, the sound of audience applause is louder (though dying)

Branston Parrish (*very pleased with himself*) Didn't they just love that? They wanted an encore, you know. But I wouldn't give it to them.
Miss Horton Why not, Mr Parrish?
Branston Parrish I didn't want to spoil the flow of Shakespeare's story.
Miss Horton Fine time to think about that.
Maud I was appalled by your behaviour, Mr Parrish. I have not seen such a shameless exhibition of stage-hogging since — since ...
Miss Horton Since your husband was alive?
Maud Yes. (*Realizing what she's said*) No, of course not. But it was an unforgivable display, Mr Parrish! *A Midsummer Night's Dream* is a play about magic, and for you to take your ass's head off in full view of the audience totally extinguished all of the magic that I and my fairies had created.
Branston Parrish But, if I'd have kept the head on, no-one would have seen all the amusing faces I was pulling during the song, would they?
Maud That is neither here nor there, Mr Parrish. You totally destroyed the magic! Good gracious, being on the same stage as you is like the worst kind of bad dream.
Branston Parrish But the audience loved it. Give the people what they want — that's the important thing in entertainment.

Harry, Monty, Gus amble on from DR, *followed by Alexandra and Miss Lydia Farrelly. They are dressed in costumes appropriate to their characters, and wear heavy make-up*

Mrs Littlehouse enters through the door DL

Branston Parrish (*seeing Mrs Littlehouse*) Constantia, O my paragon of
feminine pulchritude, didn't they just love that?
Mrs Littlehouse Well, it did seem to be appreciated, yes. But I do slightly
wonder, Branston, whether ——
Branston Parrish (*calling out to the assembled throng*) Hey, a lot of you
didn't hear the song, did you?
Lawrence (*also calling out*) I'm sure everyone's thirsty. There's lemonade
here on the piano.
Gus Wouldn't mind something stronger, but I suppose it'll have to do.

The cast gather round the piano to get their lemonade

Branston Parrish Now you'd all like to hear it, wouldn't you?
Mrs Littlehouse (*feebly*) I'm not sure that this is quite the moment,
Branston ...
Branston Parrish Of course it is, my queen of the Sultan's harem. I'll only
do the chorus, just to give them the flavour.
Miss Horton Oh, for heaven's sake!
Maud The interval's supposed to give us the opportunity to recruit our
energies.
Branston Parrish (*ignoring these complaints*) And now, ladies and
gentlemen, a great song made popular by Mr G.H. Macdermott! (*He sings
"Up Went the Price" straight away*)
> I find it hard, very, very hard
> Though every means I try,
> My living to get and keep out of debt,
> But I can't and I don't know why,
> I bought a butcher's shop last year,
> A grand one in High Street,
> Oh! dear, oh! dear, it turned out queer
> Up went the price of meat.
> Up went the price of meat, up went the price of meat,
> There's heaps of troubles on this young man's mind,
> They raised the price of meat!

*Branston Parrish finishes the song in his customary wide-armed pose. His
audience is unimpressed. Gus does a slow hand-clap*

Gus Dashed clever performance — for a shopkeeper. Shopkeeper's song,
really, ain't it? About meat.
Branston Parrish (*rather discomfited*) I think I'll have some lemonade. (*He*

moves to the piano to help himself) Need to keep my whistle wet for the songs in the next half.

Everyone bunches into groups. Harry, Monty and Gus are together, as ever. Miss Horton, Miss Sandwich and Miss Brabazon form another little group. Maud is with Alexandra and Arabella. Branston Parrish is with Mrs Littlehouse. Lawrence and Myrtle Throckmorton stand a little aloof. All drink lemonade thirstily

Daisy, Amelia and Alberta enter disconsolately through the door DL

Daisy *(to Maud, tearfully)* There's no twace of Wedvers anywhere in the woad, Mrs De Lainey .
Maud Never mind, Daisy dear. I'm sure he'll turn up.
Daisy I'm sure my wabbit's been wun over by a wotten gweat motor car.
Maud He's probably scampering around in the hall somewhere. One of the audience will find him, you mark my words.
Daisy *(gloomily)* They'll pwobably twead on him
Maud Go on, you girls have some lemonade.
Amelia ⎱
Alberta ⎰ *(together)* Ooh, yes!

Amelia and Alberta run across to the piano. Daisy follows more slowly, still upset

Lawrence gives a "This is the moment" nod to Myrtle Throckmorton and suddenly becomes very authoritative

Lawrence Ladies and gentlemen, could I have your attention, please?
Harry What's this?
Gus What the devil do you want?
Lawrence *(taking up a tray)* May I collect your lemonade glasses?
Mrs Littlehouse Very well. Here you are.
Lawrence I don't require yours, Mrs Littlehouse.
Mrs Littlehouse *(puzzled)* Oh?
Lawrence But I'll have yours, Mr Parrish.
Branston Parrish *(too puzzled to argue, and handing it across)* Very well.
Lawrence *(to Gus)* Mr Tarleton?
Gus You've got a deuced nerve. I'm not used to be ordered around by accounts clerks.
Harry Give it to him, Gus. Let him play his little games.

Gus hands his glass across with bad grace

Would you like mine too?
Lawrence Please, Mr Trunchpole.
Harry (*handing it across*) Of course.
Monty Do you want mine?
Lawrence No thank you, Mr Pottle. (*He looks hard at Lydia Farrelly*)

Lydia Farrelly turns away, embarrassed

Nor yours, Miss Farrelly.
Lydia Farrelly (*relieved*) Oh.
Lawrence (*turning to Maud*) But I would like to take yours, Mrs De Lainey.

Maud considers arguing, for a moment. But then she meekly hands her glass across

Branston Parrish I wish someone could tell me what the devil's going on here.
Lawrence All will be explained very shortly, Mr Parrish. But first, Miss Throckmorton has something to tell you all.
Gus (*sarcastically*) I'm sure anything Miss Throckmorton has to tell us will be profoundly interesting.

Myrtle Throckmorton is thrown by this, and looks across to Lawrence

Lawrence (*reassuringly*) Tell them what you have to tell them, Myrtle.
Myrtle Throckmorton Very well. (*She clears her throat*) This afternoon I have been to see the police ——

Everyone reacts in surprise

—— in connection with the murder of Mr De Lainey.

There are more reactions of surprise

The fact is —— (*she finds the next bit difficult to get out*) I had been guilty of —— telling an untruth —— about the movements of Mr Galley at the time of Mr De Lainey's death.

There are puzzled reactions

At the police station I was interviewed by a young Detective-Sergeant —— (*a little coyly*) a very charming Detective-Sergeant, as it happened, called Frobisher —— very charming indeed ——
Branston Parrish Get on with it, girl!

Myrtle Throckmorton Yes. Yes, of course. I explained to Detective-Sergeant Frobisher — well, "Frobie" he likes to be called, actually — that at the time Mr Galley was believed to have been murdering Mr De Lainey — he was in fact with me ...

Miss Horton With you? Where?

Myrtle Throckmorton (*embarrassed*) In his ... cubby-hole.

Miss Horton And might I ask, Miss Throckmorton, what you, a single lady, were doing in a cubby-hole with a convicted jewel-thief who was masquerading under a false name?

Myrtle Throckmorton (*even more embarrassed*) Well, I ...

Lawrence (*coming to her rescue*) The main point is that what Miss Throckmorton told the police means that Mr Galley could not possibly have killed Mr De Lainey.

There is a stunned reaction

Which also means that the murder was committed by somebody else.

There a loud reactions of disbelief, etc.

Maud But this is preposterous! Why should Miss Throckmorton's new story be any more truthful than her previous one? A young lady who is prepared to lie to the police should be being charged with perverting the course of justice, rather than being allowed to make accusation against innocent members of the public.

Lawrence No accusations have been made yet, Mrs De Lainey. And when she went to the police station this afternoon, Miss Throckmorton was well aware that she was risking criminal proceedings against herself.

Myrtle Throckmorton (*downcast*) Yes, and I discovered that perverting the cause of justice is a crime that carries a potential sentence of fourteen years' penal servitude. (*Perking up*) But Detective-Sergeant Frobisher did say that it might be possible for such proceedings to be avoided — if I were to give full co-operation to the police's reopened investigation. (*She blushes*) What he actually said was that I was a naughty girl and I deserved a spank-bottom ... (*Moving quickly on*) I do feel deeply sorry for my stupid lies and ——

Lawrence No time for regrets. It is more important that we unmask the true murderer of Mr De Lainey.

Branston Parrish Isn't that a job for the police, Mr Furze?

Lawrence The police will be conducting their own investigations, but I thought it might be useful to ——

Maud What you're saying is that the police haven't got any evidence against anyone else who was here on that dreadful night. They have nothing that will stand up in court.

Lawrence (*downcast*) No. You're right.

Harry Then I don't really see why we're going through this less-than-fascinating charade. There's an audience out there who can't wait to listen to more comic songs interspersed with snatches of Shakespeare.

Branston Parrish That's true. They definitely do want more of me.

The cast react; they want to get back to the play

Lawrence (*forcibly riding over this*) No! Listen! There is a way we can prove the identity of the murderer.

Branston Parrish I don't see how there can be, unless someone saw him — (*looking beadily at Maud*) or *her* ... actually doing the deed.

Lawrence There's another way. Using the latest innovation in police investigation techniques.

Monty What's that?

Lawrence Fingerprints.

Harry Oh, I've heard about this. Some deuced nonsense that everyone carries their own signature on their fingertips, and that no two people in the history of mankind have ever had the same prints.

Lawrence It's true.

Gus All sounds like arrant tosh to me.

Lawrence Well, let us put it to the test.

Branston Parrish Oh, surely we don't have to ...

Lawrence (*riding forcibly over him*) And those who have no guilty secrets have nothing to fear. Do they, Mr Parrish?

Branston Parrish (*uncomfortably*) I suppose not.

Lawrence Do you have any objections to my undertaking this experiment, Mrs De Lainey?

Maud I dare say I might have — if I understood a word you were saying. From what I have read in the newspapers, fingerprinting sounds a very messy business — immersing one's hands in great big pots of ink

Lawrence That will not be necessary today, Mrs De Lainey. I already have all the fingerprints I require.

Branston Parrish But how? None of us have got our prints on the police register, have we?

Lawrence That remains to be found out, Mr Parrish.

Branston Parrish looks uncomfortable. Lawrence takes up the powder-puff and dips it in the box of powder

As I say, I need no ink. (*Matching his actions to his words during the following*) I have the lemonade glasses of all those who had the opportunity to kill Mr De Lainey, and the lightest dusting over them with this powder will bring out the individual fingerprints with extraordinary clarity.

Harry This is all deuced clever, Mr Furze, but I don't see what use it is to us. Very well, you have our fingerprints, but so far as I can see, you have no matching fingerprints from the scene of the crime.

Lawrence (*picking up the envelope he had placed on top of the piano*) That is where you are wrong, Mr Trunchpole. My good friend, Detective-Sergeant Charles Stockley Collins of the Central Fingerprint Branch was generous enough to lend me the photographs of the prints which were on the hilt of the sword used to kill Mr De Lainey.

Harry (*rattled*) The devil he was!

Lawrence (*taking stiff photographic plates out of the envelope*) So all I have to do is to compare the prints on the photographs with these that you four have so generously donated on your lemonade glasses.

Branston Parrish This whole business is tommy-rot! It's a conjuring trick, the kind of thing Maskelyne and Cooke fool the public with at the Egyptian Hall!

Lawrence If that's so then, Mr Parrish, you have nothing to worry about, do you?

Branston Parrish (*very uncomfortably*) No.

Lawrence takes out a magnifying glass and compares the marks on one of the glasses with the photographic plate in his hand. There is silence; everyone on stage is riveted by what he is doing

Lawrence Well, Mr Parrish. You will be relieved to know that there are no points of similarity between your fingerprints and those on the murder weapon.

There are reactions of relief from everyone

Branston Parrish (*more relieved than he's admitting*) I never thought there would be.

Lawrence Now this was your glass — wasn't it, Mrs De Lainey?

Maud (*blustering*) Yes. But it'll be no surprise if you do find my fingerprints on the murder weapon. Sydney and I owned those swords. I frequently carried them around, so there can be no assumption of guilt if ——

Lawrence Well, let's just see, shall we ...? (*He compares the photograph with another of the glasses*)

Once again there is silence

(*After a moment of looking at the glass*) How long have you had that scar on your thumb, Mrs De Lainey?

Maud (*shocked that he can recognize it*) It was a childhood injury. I cut myself while peeling an apple when I was seven years old.

Lawrence Hm ...

*Lawrence looks through his magnifying glass again. There is a long silence.
Then he straightens up*

However, there is no matching scar on the thumb of your husband's
murderer.

There are reactions of relief from everyone

Maud (*pretending the tension hadn't got to her*) I could have told you that,
Mr Furze.

Maud sits down with some relief, and is comforted by her daughters

Lawrence (*turning to look at Harry and Gus*) So — it seems our investigations
are now reduced to you two gentlemen.
Harry Look. This has all been a frightfully jolly jape, Mr Furze, and we've
played along with your little fantasy, but I think it's now the time to
introduce some reality into our proceedings.
Gus Couldn't agree more, Harry.
Harry The fact is, Socialism is clearly a wonderful thing, but it can go too
far. There are rules in our society. And when you get a mere accounts clerk
insulting his betters, the time has come to draw the line.
Gus So just shift-ho — right, Mr Furze?
Lawrence I'm sorry, I won't. Mr De Lainey has been murdered, and I am
going to expose the man who committed that wicked and despicable crime.
Harry No, you're not, young shaver!

*Harry moves suddenly forwards and dashes the contents of Lawrence's tray
all over the floor. The glasses shatter. There is a reaction of shock from all
present, followed by silence*

Lawrence Mr Trunchpole, there is a general perception that the destruction
of evidence is the action of a guilty man.
Harry The devil there is! I'm not guilty. I just cannot sit by and watch a tag-
rag like you insult his betters by this ridiculous masquerade!
Gus Cut the bluster, Harry.
Harry (*surprised*) What?
Gus Can't you tell when the game's up? He's got you cornered like a fox in
a quarry.
Harry Gus ... I thought you'd stand by me.

Gus I'd have stood by you as long as there was any chance of your getting
away with it, but you can't keep on shooting when you're out of cartridges.
Do the square thing, Harry, and admit it.

Harry But ——

Gus Admit that you killed Mr De Lainey to stop him standing in the way of
your marriage to his daughter Alexandra.

There is a shocked reaction from Alexandra and Maud

(*To Lawrence*) For as long as I could, I kept up the story that Harry and I
were together in the foyer of the hall when Mr De Lainey was killed — but,
as you've shown me, Mr Furze, a chap can't maintain a lie for ever.
(*Turning to Harry*) I'm sorry, Harry. I tried to help you, but now I have to
do the decent thing.

Harry You deuced traitor! (*Leaping towards Gus*) I'll beat you to within an
inch of your life!

Lawrence Grab him!

Branston Parrish and Monty each grab one of Harry's arms and restrain him

Monty I'm dashed shocked, Harry. I always thought of you as a cricketer.
Straight bat and all that.

Harry You don't understand …

Gus I'm sorry. I think it's time the police were called. (*Making for the door
DL*) I'll go and fetch them

Lawrence (*stopping Gus in his tracks*) Just a minute, Mr Tarleton …

Gus I don't mind doing it. Glad to be of help. And at least if I go, I won't have
to stay here with that — (*looking venomously at Harry*) two-faced four-
flusher!

Lawrence (*taking some papers out of his envelope*) Thank you very much
for the offer, Mr Tarleton, but I'd like you to stay until you've heard the
details of why this murder was committed.

Gus (*undecided*) Well … (*Deciding he'll have to stay*) As you wish.

Lawrence The motive was in fact a financial one. Our murderer was up to
his neck in gambling debts.

Alexandra (*shocked*) Harry.

Monty (*to Harry*) Crikey, old man, I thought you always kept a brake on
things.

Harry But I ——

Lawrence (*overriding him*) And he saw the theft of the diamond crowns,
which necessitated the death of Mr De Lainey, as the solution to his
difficulties. (*Indicating his papers*) My contacts at Scotland Yard have
been good enough to furnish me with details of all the debts our murderer

had accumulated. More importantly, they have tracked down the fence in Limehouse to whom the two diamond crowns were sold.

Harry But I never touched the diamond crowns!

Lawrence I know you didn't, Mr Trunchpole. (*Turning to Gus*) You did, though, Mr Tarleton, didn't you?

Gus You have no proof, now Harry's smashed the lemonade glass!

Lawrence Oh, Mr Tarleton, you don't understand the beautiful simplicity of the fingerprint system. (*Indicating the smashed lemonade glasses*) We may have lost one perfect match — but we have only to dip your fingers in ink and press them or paper to find another.

Gus So ... all right. I did kill the old fool. (*Suddenly making for the door* DL) But you won't catch me! I'll go abroad! No-one will ever find me!

The door DL *opens before Gus reaches it, and Gus finds himself faced by the very considerable bulk of the uniformed Detective-Sergeant Frobisher*

At the same time Branston Parrish and Monty release their hold on Harry

Gus The devil!

Myrtle Throckmorton (*delightedly*) Frobie!

Lawrence Mr Tarleton, Detective-Sergeant Frobisher has been listening at the door since the interval started. He has heard your confession of murder. Haven't you, Detective-Sergeant Frobisher?

Detective-Sergeant Frobisher Indeed I have, sir.

Gus If I'm already damned for killing one man — (*pulling a revolver out of his tunic*) don't imagine I'd be afraid to kill more.

Everyone backs off in a circle. Gus moves US, *covering them with the gun*

Stay back! (*He gives a quick look* US, *and sees that the central doors are a little open*) I'll get out through the hall! (*He disappears behind the curtain of the men's changing compartment*)

The central doors and the two other US *doors are firmly shut*

Detective-Sergeant Frobisher It won't work, sir. I've got my men in the hall too.

Gus (*out of sight*) Dammit! All right then — if I'm to be arrested — (*he holds the curtain of the compartment closed*) somebody's going to have to come in here and get me.

Detective-Sergeant Frobisher (*moving towards the changing compartment; without great enthusiasm*) Very well. If that's what's required, I suppose ...

Myrtle Throckmorton No, don't do it, Frobie!
Lawrence (*stepping forward*) Don't worry. I'll tackle him.
Alexandra No, don't do it, Lawrence!

Lawrence looks at Alexandra. There is a moment of eye contact

Detective-Sergeant Frobisher (*stepping back towards the door* DL, *with considerable alacrity*) Well, if you don't mind — I would do it myself, of course, but, erm …
Lawrence No, I'm a great believer in finishing anything that I've s-s-s-s-s-s ——
Entire cast (*except for Gus and Harry*) Started.

Lawrence steps inside the curtained compartment, drawing the curtain closed after him

There is a tense silence

Gus (*out of sight*) Determined to be a hero, aren't you? An heroic accounts clerk. (*Viciously*) But sadly a *dead* heroic accounts clerk!

The sounds of a struggle are heard from behind the curtains, with some oaths and grunts from the two participants

The assembled throng look on, appalled

There is the sound of a gunshot. Alexandra screams

Silence descends again

The curtain twitches, and Gus comes out through a narrow gap. He is completely unharmed, and still holds his gun out in front of him, covering everyone

Alexandra Lawrence! (*She bursts into tears*) Lawrence!

Gus moves towards the door DL. *Detective-Sergeant Frobisher is still standing in front of it. Gus waves the gun at him and the policeman, deciding discretion to be the better part of valour, moves to one side*

Then, slowly, the curtain of the men's compartment is drawn back. Everyone — including Gus — watches with appalled fascination, as the opening curtain reveals — Lawrence, totally unharmed, standing there. He brings his arm round from behind his back and holds up — a dead rabbit

Daisy (*furiously angry and rushing across to attack Gus*) You wotter!
You've shot my wabbit!
Alberta You beast!

*The two little girls both hurl themselves with such force and fury at Gus's
midriff that he is totally taken off guard. His revolver flies up in the air, and
is neatly caught by Detective-Sergeant Frobisher, who trains it on him.
Branston Parrish and Monty come forward and pinion Gus's arms. Maud
comes forward, trying to drag the two little girls off their quarry*

Maud Come on, girls! That's quite enough.
Daisy No, it isn't! I weally must have one more kick at the wotten wogue!
Maud Oh, very well.

Daisy kicks Gus

Gus Ow!
Alberta And I want to give him another kick too!
Maud All right, dear. Just the one.

Alberta kicks Gus

Gus Ow! Ooh, you little monster! (*He hops about in pain*)

*Daisy and Alberta wipe their hands with the satisfaction of a job well done,
and then demurely follow Maud across the stage*

*Lawrence drops the rabbit back into the male changing compartment.
During the following, Daisy goes into that compartment*

Detective-Sergeant Frobisher So, Mr Tarleton, seems like we have to add
to your charge sheet — the murder of a rabbit.
Gus Do what you damned well like.
Detective-Sergeant Frobisher (*opening the door* DR *and calling out*) All
right, boys. I'm bringing out the prisoner. Get the van ready to receive him.

Branston Parrish and Monty lead Gus out DL

Harry (*calling after them*) Monty, see if you can sort out bail for him!
Detective-Sergeant Frobisher I don't think bail would be appropriate, sir.
This isn't one of the pranks your type usually get up to — like having a few
too many drinks on Boat Race Night. No-one's going to buy his way out
of these charges. This is a case of murder, for which the punishment is death
by hanging.

Harry (*subdued*) Yes.

Myrtle Throckmorton (*moving to Detective-Sergeant Frobisher*) Oh, Frobie ... You were so *brave* ...

Detective-Sergeant Frobisher Only in the line of duty, miss.

Myrtle Throckmorton (*holding her hands out as if she's about to be handcuffed*) And of course you've got to take me down to the station too, haven't you?

Detective-Sergeant Frobisher Why's that then?

Myrtle Throckmorton The charge of perverting the course of justice.

Detective-Sergeant Frobisher Oh, that's true. (*Putting his arm around her waist*) And while I'm at it, I might teach you a few other ways of perverting the course of justice.

Detective-Sergeant Frobisher and Myrtle Throckmorton head for the door DL

Myrtle Throckmorton Ooh, Frobie ...

They exit

Miss Horton (*to Miss Sandwich*) Well, didn't I say that would happen?

Miss Sandwich No, you didn't.

Miss Horton (*amazed at being argued with*) What?

Miss Sandwich You said nothing of the kind.

Miss Horton But I ——

Miss Sandwich, the worm turning, drives Miss Horton towards the door DR by the sheer force of her pent-up personality

Miss Sandwich You think you're always right, Miss Horton, when most of the time you're just plain, bloody wrong!

Miss Horton (*shocked*) Miss Sandwich! Do I hear the subterranean rustle of a worm turning?

Miss Sandwich Yes, you bloody do!

Miss Horton and Miss Sandwich exit through the door DR during the following

And another thing: just because *you're* a sour, desiccated old spinster, it doesn't mean that I'm the same kind of joyless, dispirited wet blanket. I have my own personality and ...

Branston Parrish enters through the door DR, rubbing his hands with glee. Monty, more subdued, follows him

Branston Parrish Do you realize something, Constantia, O my blossom of early snowdrop?

Mrs Littlehouse No, Branston.

Branston Parrish There's still an audience out there. Since the absence of a Theseus means they can no longer receive *A Midsummer Night's Dream* — we'll have to do something else for them, won't we?

Mrs Littlehouse Will we? What?

Branston Parrish It's obvious. I will sing them the *entire repertoire* of my comic songs. Now don't you think they'd like that?

Mrs Littlehouse (*not entirely sure*) Well ...

Branston Parrish (*picking up a pile of sheet music*) Come along, Miss Brabazon. You're going to play for me, aren't you?

Miss Brabazon (*on her high horse*) Mr Parrish, if you think I'm going to play profane and licentious songs for ——

Branston Parrish You'll be paid extra.

Miss Brabazon Oh, very well then.

Branston Parrish, Mrs Littlehouse and Miss Brabazon go out through the door UL

Monty (*to Harry; inadequately*) Old man, I don't know what to say ...

Harry Nothing to say. Gus was a bad lot all the time, and I never knew it.

Monty Damned bad show.

Harry Yes. Bit of a jar.

Monty Mm.

An awkward silence

By the way, Mr Furze, that was dashed clever, the drill you did with the fingerprints. I didn't realize that they'd show up like that, just with a bit of ordinary powder on a lemonade glass.

Lawrence They wouldn't.

Monty What?

Lawrence You need much more sophisticated equipment than that, special powder, all sorts.

Harry You mean you were bluffing?

Lawrence Of course I was. Took the calculated risk that it might prompt a confession and — I was right, wasn't I?

Harry (*angrily*) So Gus needn't have confessed? You actually had no evidence against him?

Lawrence None at all.

Harry Dammit! I think that's a pretty underhand way of going about things, Mr Furze!

Lawrence More underhand than lying to protect someone you know to have committed murder?

Harry Well ... (*But he really has no answer*)

Lydia Farrelly comes across to rescue Monty from the awkwardness

Lydia Farrelly Monty, since we've finished early ...

Monty Yes, my angel?

Lydia Farrelly We've actually got some time — to go out and have some dinner — if we wanted to.

Monty Wouldn't mind. I'm deuced peckish. Anywhere you fancy going?

Lydia Farrelly There's a place I've heard of — in the Strand. Never been there, of course, but I'm told the — food's very good.

Monty What's it called?

Lydia Farrelly I think it's — Romano's ...

Monty Ah. (*Very enthusiastically*) Yes, that's just the ticket! (*He gives Harry a gleeful look*)

Harry nods ruefully

I think, Lydia, it's about time I introduced you to the full delights of Romano's ... Cheerio, everyone.

Monty and Lydia Farrelly set off for the door DL

(*Rubbing his hands together*) Yes, I think this could be the night.

Lydia Farrelly (*innocently*) And Romano's *is* the kind of place a lady of my reputation can appear without a chaperone, I trust?

Monty You'll be fine, my angel, in my capable hands.

Lydia Farrelly (*as they go; with a slightly less innocent giggle*) Ooh, Monty ...

Monty and Lydia Farrelly exit

Lawrence and Harry stand awkwardly one side of the stage, Maud with her daughters on the other side

Arabella I wonder how far they'll have got before they realize they're still in costume.

Harry I can assure you Monty won't be the only fairy at Romano's.

Maud (*after giving him a withering look*) I think we'd better be going, girls. It's just as well we changed into our costumes at home. Where's Daisy?

Daisy (*solemnly emerging from the male compartment carrying a little bundle wrapped in a shawl*) I'm weady. I've got Wedvers with me.

Maud Good. Come along then.

Alexandra I'm going to stay for a while, Mama.

Maud (*bossily*) Alexandra, you will come with me when I ——

Alexandra (*gently but firmly*) Mama, I am going to stay for a while.

Maud (*recognizing her daughter's superior will*) Very well, Alexandra. I will see you later. Now come along, girls.

Alexandra moves across towards Lawrence and Harry

Maud leads her remaining girls and Daisy towards the door DL

Daisy I'm going to give Wedvers a pwoper state funewal.

Alberta Yes, just like Queen Victoria's. I'm sure we can get some gun-carriages from somewhere ...

Maud, Alberta and Daisy exit. Arabella lingers for a moment, waves luck to Alexandra, and then exits

There is a moment of awkwardness between the three left on stage

Lawrence Why did you cover up for him, Mr Trunchpole? Why didn't you tell the truth?

Harry A chap doesn't rat on one of his own kind.

Lawrence Well, you've just had a very good example of Mr Tarleton's ratting on you.

Harry Yes, it's ... I don't think you'd understand, Mr Furze. It's a matter of the way one's brought up.

Lawrence I was brought up to tell the truth.

Alexandra And so was I.

Harry Hm. Well, I suppose this is goodbye — isn't it, Alex?

Alexandra Yes.

Harry (*going to pick up his normal clothes from inside the men's changing compartment*) There are lots of things I could say that ——

Alexandra Don't say any of them.

Harry No. Very well. Goodbye. (*He heads for the door* DL *singing softly to himself*) Bill Bailey, won't you please come home ...?

Harry exits

Lawrence and Alexandra look at each other

Alexandra I was so proud of you, Lawrence, so proud.

Lawrence Thank you.

Alexandra And so terrified that he might have shot you. I realized at that moment that I couldn't face the prospect of life without you, Lawrence.
Lawrence And I couldn't face the prospect of life without you, Alexandra.

They hold hands and stare soupily at each other. Distantly from the hall comes the sound of Branston Parrish's voice

Branston Parrish (*off*) Now here's one I'm sure you know. It's a ladies' song but we'll sing it all together now.

Branston leads the offstage audience in singing "The Boy I Love Is Up In The Gallery"

Branston Parrish ⎱ I'm a young girl and have just come over,
Audience ⎰ Over from the country where they do things big;
And amongst the boys I've got a lover,
And since I've got a lover, why I don't care a fig!

Chorus

The boy I love is up in the gallery,
The boy I love is looking now at me;
There he is, can't you see? Waving his handkerchief,
As merry as a robin that sings on the tree.

The boy I love they call him a cobbler,
But he's not a cobbler, allow me to state;
For Johnny is a tradesman, and he works in the Boro',
Where they sole and heel them whilst you wait.

Chorus

The boy I love ... *etc.*

Lawrence (*breaking free embarrassed and moving* US) Sounds like Branston's got them all singing. (*He opens the door* UC)

The sound of Branston Parrish's and the audience's singing is louder

(*Awkwardly*) He's certainly got them all singing.
Alexandra (*holding her hand out to him*) Lawrence.
Lawrence (*coming to take Alexandra's hand*) Yes, Alexandra.

They look at each other soupily

I say — would you like to do something for me?

Alexandra I'm sure I would. What would you like me to do for you, Lawrence?

Lawrence (*having difficulty getting the words out*) I'd like you to ... I'd like you to ... Alexandra ... (*In a rush*) Would you take me with you to a lecture by Mr George Bernard Shaw?

Alexandra Of course I would, Lawrence.

Lawrence And — one other thing ...

Alexandra Mm.

Lawrence I was very silly about it last time. I felt guilty and stupid and — Alexandra, would you mind kissing me?

Alexandra No, Lawrence, I wouldn't mind at all.

Alexandra kisses Lawrence, gently at first. Then they go into a big clinch as the singing of "The Boy I Love Is Up in the Gallery" from the hall wells up

The CURTAIN *falls*

FURNITURE AND PROPERTY LIST

ACT I
SCENE 1

On stage: Gaslights
Large portrait of Queen Victoria
Plaques
Large committee table
Matching chairs
Upright piano

Off stage: Lighted taper (**Mr Galley**)
Ping-Pong set: box containing bats, net, celluloid balls (**Harry**)
Two books (**Lawrence Furze**)
Box of playscripts (**Mr Galley**)

Personal: **Harry**: coin
Branston Parrish: *The Times*

SCENE 2

Strike: Committee table
Ping-Pong set
Portrait of Queen Victoria

Set: Portrait of King Edward VII garlanded with red, white and blue ribbons

Off stage: Smart wooden box containing two tiaras, large cardboard box containing stage ass's head, two swords (**Mrs Littlehouse**)
Dressing-room structure: two outer panels, central panel, central dividing panel (cloth), cross-strut, pair of curtains (**Gus, Harry, Monty, Mr Galley**)
Costumes (**Mrs Littlehouse and Myrtle Throckmorton**)
Wicker animal basket (**Daisy**)

Personal: Blood capsule, replica of sword to protrude from chest (**Sydney De Lainey**)

ACT II
SCENE 1

Re-set: Open all curtains on dressing-room structure

Set: *The Times* newspaper on chair

Strike: Red, white and blue ribbons, boxes, swords, ass's head, costumes

Off stage: Book (**Lawrence**)
                 Animal baskets (**Amelia, Alberta, Daisy**)

SCENE 2

Re-set: Close all curtains on dressing-room structure, open doors to hall
                 slightly

Set: Jug of lemonade and glasses on a tray on piano
                 In male changing-compartment: envelope of papers and photographic
                     plates, dead rabbit for **Lawrence**, bundle in shawl for **Daisy**
                 In female changing-compartment: powder and powder-puff for **Myrtle
                     Throckmorton**

Personal: Magnifying glass (**Lawrence**)
                 Revolver (**Gus**)

LIGHTING PLOT

Practical fittings required: "gas-lights"
One interior with window backing. The same throughout

ACT I, Scene 1

To open: Darkness

Cue 1	**Mr Galley** lights the gas-lights in order from L *Bring up lights gradually from* L	(Page 1)
Cue 2	**Sydney De Lainey**: "... O, methinks, how slooooow ..." *Fade slowly*	(Page 32)

ACT I, Scene 2

To open: Late afternoon lighting on window backing; gas-lights on

No cues

ACT II, Scene 1

To open: Daytime lighting on window backing; gas-lights on

No cues

ACT II, Scene 2

To open: Darkness outside windows; gas-lights on

No cues

EFFECTS PLOT

ACT I

Cue 1   **Mrs Littlehouse**: " ... written by William Shakespeare."   (Page 21)
Sound of 1902 motor car approaches from L

Cue 2   **Monty**: "What a scorcher!"   (Page 21)
Car brakes and stops and engine noise ceases

ACT II

Cue 3   **Lawrence**: " ... shred of actual evidence that ——"   (Page 60)
Sound of 1902 motor car approaches from L; *stops*

Cue 4   **Miss Horton**: " ... as much as I can tolerate."   (Page 76)
Sound of enthusiastic applause, tailing off slowly

Cue 5   **Branston Parrish** bursts in   (Page 77)
Increase sound of dying applause while door is open

Cue 6   Sounds of struggle behind curtains   (Page 87)
Gunshot

Cue 7   **Branston Parrish**: " ... all together now."   (Page 93)
Branston and **Audience** sing "The Boy I Love Is Up
In The Gallery"

Cue 8   **Lawrence** opens the door uc   (Page 93)
Branston's *and* **Audience**'s *singing louder*

Cue 9   **Alexandra** and **Lawrence** go into a big clinch   (Page 94)
Singing wells up louder